GOODYEAR

#1 in Tires

TIRE WARS

TIRE WARS
RACING WITH GOODYEAR

William Neely

with foreword by

Chris Economaki

AZTEX Corporation
Tucson, AZ 85703

VERSO

ISBN 0-89404-091-X

Library of Congress Catalog Card No. 93-072137

Printed in the United States of America

AZTEX Corporation
P O Box 50046, Tucson, AZ 85703-1046

Arizona Historical Society Library
AZTEX Corporation
Cahier, Bernard
Charlotte Motor Speedway
Darlington International Raceway
Goodyear Tire & Rubber Company
Institute of Gas Technology
International Motor Sports Association
International Speedway Corp/NASCAR
Mercedes-Benz of North America, Inc.
National Speed Sport News
Pennzoil Corporation
Penske Corporation

This one's for you,
Whitney, my love

Chris Economaki, publisher emeritus of National Speed Sport News, *has been covering racing events as both writer and broadcaster for about fifty years.*

As motorsports gains in popularity year after year, so too does interest in its beginnings and in its 100-year history. It is a saga that winds from 1895, when the very first race was held in Chicago, until today when 400,000 jubilant fans jam the Indianapolis Motor Speedway on Memorial Day weekend, cheering wildly for their favorite driver as television cameras and radio microphones carry the tale of the race to fans throughout the entire world.

As complex as racing may seem to the neophyte, it really has but three basic ingredients: the cars, the drivers, and the course on which the race is run. The link between the car and driver is obvious, consisting of a steering wheel, a seat and three pedals.

The link between the car and driver and the road is a much more tenuous affair. The surface can be rough or smooth, dry or wet, hot or cold—or any combination of these; but no matter what, the car must maintain adhesion, often at speeds above 200 miles per hour, or the result is disaster.

The job of maintaining a grip on the road is where Goodyear comes in, and where the pacesetting company has been involved from the earliest stages of automobile racing. The Wingfoot Clan has been ever-present in the quest for faster speeds and safer conditions. From the days of the demountable rim and the clincher tire, right up to today's trouble-free tubeless designs, Goodyear has been up to its corporate ears in its laboratories and on the racing circuits of the world.

Racing perfection has been a never-ending quest for Goodyear, measured at times by successes in the laboratory, at others by a checkered flag and still at other times by the confidence the name Goodyear instills in someone considering new tires for the family sedan. The fact that more checkered flags have fallen on Goodyear-shod cars than on any other brand in the world helps to inspire this reliance.

It has been a laborious struggle to reach the pinnacle of international racing, but Goodyear has made it. This is the dramatic and fascinating story of how and why it all happened. I was there for half a century of it and I have marvelled at the company's tenacity and integrity. Now you have an opportunity to be there (and for the other half century). I hope you enjoy the book as much as I did.

Chris Economaki

Motorsports wouldn't be where it is today without the Wingfoot

William Neely, better known around race tracks as Bill, has been covering major racing events and personalities for major magazines and books since 1960.

There was no way Goodyear could lose the Indianapolis 500 or the Daytona 500 or The International Race of Champions or *any* Formula I or Winston Cup race in 1992, for that matter.

The reason was simple: Every car in the races ran on time-proven and celebrated Goodyear Eagles—the most famous tire ever built—for road or track.

How the tires became so successful and would, within a matter of a few years after Goodyear really got serious, totally drive away from the world's racing scene such worthy and primeval competition as Firestone, Michelin, Dunlop and Pirelli, was *far* from simple. In fact, it is a tangible tribute to the determination, devotion and excellence of the men of the company's engineering, development, testing and racing divisions.

A.J. Foyt Jr. played a vital role in the upward surge of the company's tires when, in 1963, he stomped to a phone booth, upset with Firestone, and asked Goodyear engineers to "bring some of your tires down here." They scurried to Indy with a passel of wide Stock Car Special tires, only to find out that it would take some serious design, compounding and testing to compete with Firestone at the "brickyard," where their cross-town rivals had ruled for decades and, after all, had all the experience in the world. They were a formidable foe.

Craig Breedlove added another nail to the competition's coffin when he brought the World Land Speed Record back to the United States in an appropriately-named vehicle, *The Spirit of America.*

But it was long before the Indianapolis 500 in 1963 when the desire and determination were instilled in the hearts of Goodyear tire-builders. Long before.

It was even before Tim and Fonty Flock won several NASCAR races in 1955 in Carl Kiekhaefer-prepared Chryslers or before Lee Petty tested wider and faster—and safer—stock car racing tires at a tiny track in West Palm Beach, Florida, in 1957. Because of the Petty tests, Buck Baker won the NASCAR championship that year on Goodyears. Drivers had already begun to trust the Wingfoot.

It was all uphill, flat-out and belly to the ground after the Petty testing and the Baker championship.

It began long before they were born. The spirit of speed within the company went back beyond the 1919 Indy 500 when Howdy Wilcox won the American classic on Goodyear cords. You see, that year the company dominated the sport, winning every major race in the country. It only goes to prove that there is a spirit and always has been—pride, if you please—that lurks within the breast of every Goodyear associate, a determination that calls for winning when the chips are down.

Barney Oldfield was the first race driver to reach "household word" status, and he did it on Goodyears in 1905 and 1906 by setting a string of records, one of which still stands nearly a century later. Oldfield *and* the tires were famous. I could rest my case there, but that's merely the beginning, so as Paul Harvey might say, "Let's hear the rest of the story." It's an American saga.

First Efforts

It wasn't even Oldfield who got Goodyear's interest aroused.

If one was hard-pressed to pick the actual time when the spirit began to take wings, it probably would have been in 1901 when Henry Ford and Charles Seiberling, Goodyear's sales manager and brother of the company's founder, worked out a deal to use Goodyear tires on the aboriginal Ford racing cars. Seiberling magnanimously sold Mr. Ford a set of tires. At cost. Racing was young and finding anyone even willing to *try* was next to impossible. Henry the First took him up on it.

The art of tire-building was in a primitive, almost monolithic, stage at the time. Nevertheless, Goodyear associates hand-built—as they did all tires—a set of "racing" tires for Mr. Ford *Himself*. It was a very special set. Every visible and manual means of examining the components and assembling them was used; it was a real, live case of "making clothes for the emperor."

Seiberling obviously recognized, as did Ford, that the race course was precisely the place to test tire and car. "If they do well on a race course, then we expect them to do even better on the nation's roads," said Seiberling. It made him somewhat of a sage. The race track was the perfect place to test the comparative excellence of tires of the period, not to mention dependability for the four patches of rubber that touched the road—the final and most important link between the car and the surface upon which it rode, even though it was dirt. The desire to build the best was present in the minds of both men.

This rudimentary beginning placed an undisputed desire in the hearts of Goodyear executives and employees for decades to come. And, although actual competition was placed on the back burner for a few years, the craving grew, and reached fruition with a vengeance in the Sixties. The desire to drive all others from racing reached fever pitch at Goodyear's headquarters on East Market Street in Akron.

Unwittingly, the Ford-Seiberling deal was the beginning of a glorious future that was to come to Goodyear.

Reawakening the Competitive Spirit

By 1960 there already had been several NASCAR victories and an attempt was being readied for an assault on the World Land Speed Record. Dead aim was being taken on racing supremacy. The cross hairs were lined up squarely upon Goodyear's intra-city adversary Firestone—"Brand X," as they called them.

There was little question in anyone's mind that the time had come to take on the guys in red. At first, it was as if Firestone had drawn a line in the dirt and dared anyone to cross it. Goodyear not only intended to cross the line but to do it with such fervor that it would be erased forever, so that future generations of race fans would never even know the line had been there in the first place.

The four decade domination "Brand X" held on Indianapolis was a constant source of irritation, particularly the double-page spread which appeared each June in *The Saturday Evening Post, Life* and a bunch of other magazines of the period. Goodyear executives had to bite their tongues more than once in the locker room of Akron's posh Portage Country Club as their Firestone counterparts flaunted their string of Indy 500 victories that went back, uninterrupted, to 1920.

This may well have been the catalyst because board chairman

Russell DeYoung and president Victor Holt eagerly approved almost any request for racing development money. The clouds of war loomed heavily on the horizon, and, although Firestone had experienced guns, Goodyear had a stouthearted crew of dedicated and determined racing recruits, associates who had transferred from other departments to help with the battle.

They began to fashion their own arsenal.

Nobody knew much about building racing tires, including Firestone. Oh, the tires they had built for so many years for Indy were good for their time, but time was zinging past them. Speeds were increasing; new "hot shoes" were setting records everywhere they raced, despite the fact that the drivers were getting a lot of the same old thing so far as racing rubber was concerned. It can happen when you're the only game in town.

The sport welcomed with open arms this invasion—although a small assault at first. Firestone watched with a sort of bemused dread—they felt far from threatened. But within a relatively short time, they knew this was no bluff. The boys with the Blue Streaks had brought their lunch. They had come to play.

Battles Won and Lost

The tire war—the big one—ended a couple of decades ago and, with the exception of some minor outbreaks, racing has for nearly twenty years been the domain of Goodyear. Almost all of the original cast of characters are gone now. And most of the fun. The joy of grappling to the top was a whole lot more exciting than was the view once there.

But getting there—well, that's what this book is all about. So fasten your seat belts, because we're about to take a wild ride, a high-speed trip through racing history. Our vehicle? The Goodyear Wingfoot, of course. Motorsports wouldn't be where it is today without it.

Bill Neely

TABLE of CONTENTS

Mexican Road Races of the Fifties are impetus to Goodyear's return to racing.

In the mountains above Pueblo, the narrow ribbon of road the Mexicans call the Pan American Highway lurches to the left, swings back hard to the right and then straightens out for a mile or so. Aside from a few places in the lowlands, it was about the only spot on the North American continent where race cars—huge American stock sedans and sporty European roadsters alike—could run flat out. The time was the early Fifties and the race was the Mexican Road Race.

Curtis Turner, left, and Bill France tune the engine prior to the 1952 Mexican Road Race. The pair brought the Nash home in first place in the demanding and dangerous trip through the Mexican mountains and deserts but were disqualified for switching cars in mid-race.

It was a grueling test of man and machine—and tires. It also probably was what caused Goodyear to glance again toward motorsports after an absence from competition of nearly three decades. Because, you see, a Goodyear-clad car had won the Indianapolis 500 in 1919. But three years later the company quit racing. For no apparent reason.

Now, in one of the world's most arduous events, Goodyear was back—not by executive decision, by any means—but they were back nonetheless. They were there due largely to the reputation of Goodyears on the street. *Street tires!* On their own, drivers had selected Goodyears for a number of cars in the spectacular race. They were on some of the Hudsons and the Lincolns—the favorites—as well as of the sports cars.

They were not on the Ford that roared down out of the mountain pass toward Oaxaca, but what happened to that car might have had a tremendous effect on the future of all auto racing from that time on. As the car careened wildly out of a right-hander and headed for the straightaway section of road, its tires were smoking, super-heated from the corners. Half-way down the straight, the right front tire exploded and

In the fourth running of the Carrera-Pan Americana—the Mexican Road Race—Lincoln won first through fourth places in the International Large Stock Car class, for the second time in a row, and went on to win it again in 1954. Chuck Stevenson and Clay Smith were the winning drivers, covering the 1,912 miles in 20 hours, 31 minutes, 32 seconds, for an average speed of 93.02 mph.

the car spun twice, finally coming to a stop with the front end hanging precariously over a cliff. The sound of that exploding tire was heard half a hemisphere away. A wire service photo of the dramatic event appeared on the sports page of the *Akron Beacon Journal.*

There are several accounts of why Goodyear decided to begin dabbling once more with racing, but the one that seems to persist most is that company officials, seeing the photo of the car dangling over the cliff, decided it was time—given the fact that a lot of the other cars were on Goodyears—that auto racing had a better and safer tire.

So, on an informal basis, working on racing tires whenever they could find time to pull away from their passenger car, truck, or tractor tire duties (which often was evenings and weekends), they began developing what was to be a primitive version of what we know today as the *Goodyear Eagle*, the most-respected line of tires in the annals of motorsports.

Jim Loulan was the first compounder; Gene McMannis, the first racing-tire designer. As they got more help, they began the long and tedious trial-and-error process of building a safer race track tire.

By 1956, the Goodyear price catalog had a page titled: "Blue Streak Special." The description of the tire read: "The Blue Streak is Goodyear's new miracle-strength tire designed expressly for super-high-speed driving. It has exceptional handling ease and stability under extreme cornering and high-speed conditions. The engineering features include: tough, abrasion-resistant rubber, a special tread design for greater surface traction and more even tread wear, and a 6-ply 3-T Triple-Tempered nylon cord body, which gives the tire strength and less heat build-up."

The only hint that these tires were built for racing was the warning, "Confidential Owner/Driver Schedule" at the top of the page. There was a long road ahead of them.

Time passed, and Goodyear tires improved year after year. A crescendo of sorts was reached at the 1975 Indianapolis 500—*every* car in the race was shod with Goodyear Eagles—a fitting tribute to the supremacy of Goodyear racing tires. Tire problems were almost a thing of the past. What a journey it had been since the days of Goodyear Cords.

Gene McMannis, 1959, was another early Goodyear racing expert.

Earliest Racing Involvement

But we're getting ahead of our story. Let's return to those thrilling days of yesteryear, on the back of a mighty steel horse with the speed of light. In the words of Lewis Carroll: "Let us begin at the beginning:"

The place was the forerunner of the New York Auto Show—the International Exposition of the Automobile. It was one year into the Twentieth Century. Oddly, there were dozens of makes of automobiles there and even more car-builders, including one lean and resolute man from Michigan—Henry Ford.

The Ford automobile had been in existence for only a few years but it was one of the best-known and best-selling cars in America. Its image was one of dependability (which was a relative term at the turn of the century, because to *complete* a day's journey was the benchmark of any car in those days).

Ford wanted to change that image, because underneath that celluloid collar and starched white shirt beat the heart of an adventurer. His easy manner and dapper appearance belied his fierce competitive nature. He wanted his cars to be known for their dash as well as their dependability. The bottom line: speed. And the truth of the matter is that Mr. Ford lived a kind of Walter Mitty dream. He imagined himself behind the wheel of a car hurtling along at, say, a mile a minute. Actually he wanted to go *two* miles a minute, but, after all, he was realistic. That would come. He was willing to take it one step at a time.

It was fortunate for Ford that he ran into a familiar face, that of Charles Seiberling, the brother of Frank A. Seiberling, founder of The Goodyear Tire & Rubber Company. His company, which had been named for Charles Goodyear, the man who accidentally discovered the vulcanization process for rubber and made it possibly the world's most useful substance at the time, was housed in a small plant on a dusty street in Akron, Ohio.

F.A. Seiberling, president and general manager of The Goodyear Tire & Rubber Company in 1915.

Akron was then a two-day journey from Detroit, where the Ford plant sat on yet another dusty street. It was nearly as inauspicious as Goodyear's operation. But it was Mr. Ford's dream to shorten this distance, as well as the remoteness between *any* two points. Obviously, speed was the answer.

But Ford was more interested in another form of speed. Racing. The word, even then, was magic to automobile buffs. As the two men exchanged ideas, a thought struck Seiberling. Why not put Goodyear tires on one of Ford's cars and see how well they would do under such stress? Nobody had ever offered to assist Ford in his vision of fast cars; he had said that, but Seiberling didn't make any offer to help. But not at that point.

It was not a time for frivolity, especially in this early stage of motoring, so Seiberling filed away Ford's comments and when he got back to Akron, he wrote a letter to his new-found friend in Detroit. "I am willing to throw away the profit on a set of tires in order to get you started and give you a chance to test them." If necessity is the mother of invention, then surely frugality is a first cousin. But the 38-year-old Ford had little more than his plans for a new car. He figured racing would bring enough attention to what he wanted to do that money might be easier to come by. He was right.

Racing was the catalyst Ford needed to get his company on the move. On a warm July day in 1901, Henry Ford drove a car that was to become famous—old *999*—to victory on the Detroit Driving Club's one-mile oval at Grosse Pointe. The one thousand dollar first prize was all he needed to get started on his new car.

Ford retired from racing, devoting his time to car-building.

Automobiles and Competition

Nobody is sure when the first automobile race occurred, but it certainly must have been the first time two "horseless carriages" got together. Insurance historians insist that in 1894 there were but two cars in the state of Ohio. By mail they agreed to meet at a certain spot near Dayton. As the two men talked and compared machines, the talk undoubtedly turned to speed. Which motorized buckboard was faster?

So, in a slightly rolling meadow in central Ohio, perhaps the first American automobile race was held. The scenario might have unfolded earlier in a field in France. Or England. Nobody knows for sure. One thing is certain, the first event began as a challenge and as a display of pride for one's particular brand of automobile.

Insurance records indicate that the meeting in the Ohio pasture was the first damage claim. You guessed it, with but two cars in the entire state of Ohio, they ran into one another. If nothing else, it began a haggling between motorist and insurance company that continues to this very day.

Unknowingly, the two men in that Ohio field were setting the stage for a century of automobile competition. They were, in fact, creating the Foyts and the Unsers and the Pettys, who would come along a couple of generations later.

Most historians agree that the first *organized* race occurred on July 22, 1894, with a race in France, from Paris to Rouen, an astounding distance of seventy-seven miles. Race organizers agonized over whether or not *any*body would show up. But it was predictable. More than one hundred gathered, ready to do battle.

When the dust had lifted, the winning car covered the distance, averaging a blazing eleven miles per hour.

Automobile racing was born.

This first primitive event was, in many ways, a prophesy of things to come. There were bent fenders, broken cars, arguments and, at the end, a trophy, which is basically what men and women have been racing for ever since. Granted, prize money helps, but few would race if it weren't for the sheer thrill of victory.

The Paris to Rouen race touched off a craze in France of racing from city to city. In 1895, a three-day, 732-mile race was held from Paris to Bordeaux and back. The following year brought about the first *real* endurance race—1,063 miles from Paris to Marseilles and back. In terms of race car construction, it would be akin to racing to the moon and back today.

By the turn of the century, racing had taken on regulations. It brought a certain degree of order out of what had been chaos, and, in so doing, brought protests. Rules indeed. Even the Roman chariot races didn't have *rules*.

The Gordon Bennett Cup, held in France from 1900 to 1906, was the forerunner of today's Formula One series because it pitted the best drivers from many nations in competition which carried a world driving championship with it. A trophy was one thing, but being named the "best in the world" really was what set the racing wheels in motion.

World Land Speed racing began two years before the Gordon Bennett Cup. They didn't know what to call it, but again France was the spot. For one thing, they had the best roads in the world, stretching out like spokes from the hub of a wheel, the hub, quite naturally, being Paris. In 1898, just north of Paris, a vehicle blazed through a straight, measured kilometer at a speed just under forty miles per hour. It had been a flying

A Look at the Future of Racing

Memorial Day, 1982: this was the race Indy fans had waited 66 years for. With tires and cars dead equal, the contest was truly among the drivers. Gordon Johncock, who was 45 years old at the time, and who had begun racing when Rick Mears was four, suddenly was having to use all of his experience, cunning and guile to keep the young Mears at bay. Mears had roared to a new qualifying record of 207.004, so Johncock's task was not an easy one; experience or not, it's difficult to overcome sheer speed. And Mears was hunting down Johncock as the race waned.

In a nutshell, it was Mears playing the same tactical game he played until his retirement in 1992. His strategy was, don't race with them; stay in the lead lap and wait until the last pit stop. And then race with them. It's exactly what he did.

A.J. Foyt was in his 25th race and had set records for the first twenty laps. Then Tom Sneva led. Johncock had overcome handling problems about midway through the race, but he took the lead on Lap 160 and held it through a timed final pit stop at Lap 183, while Mears's crew topped-off his fuel tank

Continued on page 22

start, but a new breed of sports fanatic—the racing fan—had been born, because the fans considered forty miles per hour to be an astounding feat. There wasn't a horse around that could beat that. For any period of time, at least. By 1902 cars were sporting more powerful engines, particularly the European makes, and tires were becoming a problem. They weren't built for extreme speed, particularly when the goal suddenly became one hundred miles per hour! "Impossible," grumbled European tiremakers. "It's not impossible," cried the race drivers. I mean, these were brave men because even the best of the rolling stock at that stage was little more than a motorized version of the buckboard. Goodyear waited. And listened.

Cord tire, 1916, with all-weather tread.

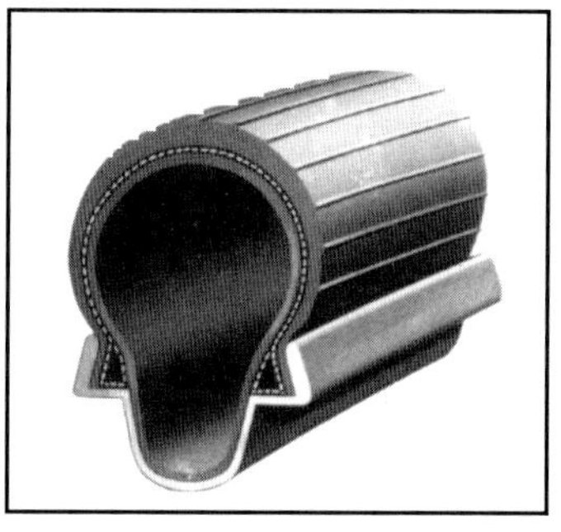
Cutaway of Bartlett's clincher tire from 1892. The basic clincher design was used by Goodyear for a number of years.

The company finally allowed a few of their tires to be used in competitive events, but with increased speeds the first pitfalls of racing appeared. In 1902 several of Goodyear's Side Flange Detachable tires disintegrated internally during a big race in England. Things had been going well when, suddenly at the speeds of more than fifty miles per hour, there was rubber and spinning cars everywhere. The very tire that had been designed and patented as the "safe tire," had its limits.

But Goodyear wasn't alone. Both Dunlop and Michelin had tire problems. It may have been the very time when the phrase "back to the drawing board" was coined.

Back in Akron, it was determined that the problem was a deficiency in the square-woven fabric used in the tires of that era. The increased flexing of the sidewalls on the race course at high speeds caused the canvas-like fabric to saw against itself until it tore. And then the tire came apart, resulting in some hair-raising moments for drivers and fans.

It was then, in 1902, that Goodyear made the first improvement in tire development—a switch to cord fabric. And it surely was the first time that the race track proved to be beneficial to the passenger car; after that, all Goodyear tires were constructed with cord fabric.

With cord fabric the strands were laid side by side and held together with rubber, preventing the cords from sawing and increasing the dependability of the tire immensely.

By 1905, Goodyear, constantly aware of the need for improved tires, pioneered a brand new auto tire concept, the Straight Side Detachable. It was a design that was not unlike the basic shape of today's tires. The company actually developed the tire to break a strangling patent on older designs, not realizing until the new tire was built and tested that they had come up with one of the most significant improvements in the history of tire design.

But it was an idea that needed to be "sold" to the motoring public, most of whom still weren't completely convinced of the notion of machine over horse. So they turned to famed race driver Barney Oldfield to help them prove their new product.

Berna Eli Oldfield was a showman, a rich one to boot, who specialized in dirt track racing. Not having the luxury of the long straight roads in France, Americans had turned to horse tracks, mostly at fairgrounds, and this is where the first racing stars began to shine.

Barney Oldfield was the best of the best. He was born in Ohio, and left school when he was twelve. After trying his hand at several jobs he took up bicycle racing, where he became an immediate success because of his "daring and dauntless style." "He has no knowledge of the word 'fear,' " said one observer.

In 1902, at the age of twenty-four, he got a break that would rocket him into the international limelight; a fellow bike racer, Tom Cooper, lent him a gasoline-powered vehicle—a racing bike—to race in his new-found home, Salt Lake City, Utah. To say that Oldfield took to it like a duck takes to water would be an understatement. He won every race in and around Salt Lake City.

Later that year he received a phone call from Cooper. It seems that he and a man by the name of Ford were building two race cars. "Would you like to drive one?" inquired Cooper. Of course that was an opportunity Oldfield couldn't turn down, so he moved back east where the cars were being built.

It was at this point that America had its first racing hero. Oldfield drove *999* and later the Winton Bullet, the Peerless Dragon and finally Walter Christie's front drive racer.

On Memorial Day 1903, Barney Oldfield became the first American to cover a mile in one minute during a match race at the Empire City horse track in New York. It was an achievement that further secured his link to fame.

He toured the country, giving exhibition runs and match races—and making a lot of money because he was almost unbeatable on any circuit. Showmanship was his theme and he became famous as an extroverted, cigar-chewing entertainer who often shouted to his fans, "You know me, I'm Barney Oldfield!" He even played briefly in a theater presentation, where he revved up his race car on stage on a treadmill and showered his delighted audience with dirt to give them the dusty road effect. More than one theater-goer refused to wash off the dirt for days, proudly proclaiming to anyone who would listen, "Barney Oldfield sprayed this dirt on me."

Oldfield was a natural to test Goodyear's new tire, and test it he did. He won seventy-two consecutive races over a fifteen month period and set every world circular track record from one to fifty miles. Without a single tire problem. Two of the tires, one front and one rear, were used for the entire fifteen months, being touched only for inflation.

This spectacular string of victories occurred during 1905-06, an era when the average tire used in racing was worn through to the cords after fifteen *miles* of intense competition.

Goodyear's racing cords were the talk of race drivers and fans throughout the country.

A Rash of Speed Record Attempts

It was at this stage that Henry Ford came out of retirement for one more speed attempt. He roared into the headlines. With his experience at building fast cars and equipping them with fast tires, he had produced a splendid machine, and he literally burst to a world land speed record of 91.370 miles per hour. It was 1904 and competition was running rampant. At every street corner and on every country lane, races were sprouting up. But the most amazing thing about Ford's achievement was that he piloted his trusty *999* to the record speed in the dead of winter. On Michigan's frozen Lake St. Clair.

Ford's record remained intact for ten days—only to be shattered at Ormond Beach, Florida, a few miles north of Daytona Beach—which, suddenly, was the mecca for speed freaks from all over the world. In 1905, an official "Speed Contest" was announced. Entries poured in from all corners of the earth. It was a year for many firsts. Oldfield took another step toward becoming a household word as he roared up and down the beach; Walter Christie entered his front-wheel-drive car with transverse-mounted engine and when he was taunted with words such as, "Come on, Walter, that type of car will never work," he left in a huff

Continued from page 20

unnecessarily. It was a slow pit stop. Johncock came in on Lap 186, took on a splash of fuel and was right back out.

Mears went back to the track, turning laps at speeds of over 200 mph, clipping off more than one second per lap on Johncock. He waited to pounce on Gordy. It was sort of like shooting fish in a barrel, he felt. But it wasn't to be that easy.

Mears drew dead abreast of Johncock on Lap 198. He went inside but had to back off. He lost a few yards, as the veteran slammed the door on him in Turn One. As the white flag waved, Mears again went inside; once more Johncock closed the door in Turn One. And again in Turn Three.

Mears pulled alongside in the front straightaway, but Johncock was determined. He held his ground, and the pair flashed under the checkered flag, with Johncock only a few feet ahead of the implacable Californian.

After the race, Mears pulled into the pits, took off his helmet and sat there. Grinning. To him it wasn't the money nor the prestige of winning the race; it was the ecstasy of battle.

The following night at the Victory Banquet, Mears received his prize money first. He turned to Johncock and told him how much fun he had had. Johncock sat there with a Jack Palance grin

Continued on page 24

and promptly invented the first army tank, which, incidentally was and, for the most part, still is a front-drive machine with its engine transverse-mounted. Seventy years later a majority of the cars were of that configuration. Ford was there with a six-cylinder vehicle; the first steam car, a streamlined automobile, was entered by Louis Ross; the first one-hundred-mile-per-hour mark was recorded; the first fatality was registered, and the very first dispute over rules was registered. It truly was "the week that was."

Bostonian H.L. Bowden, driving a monstrous twin-engined Mercedes, became the first man in America to surpass the magical one-

Henry Ford (with goggles) at Ormond Beach in 1905, with his six cylinder racer No. 666 in the background being worked on by Ford's first factory team.

hundred-mile-per-hour mark as he roared through the traps at Ormond Beach at an unfathomable 109.75. But Arthur MacDonald drove his British Napier to a 104.65 mpg average, and then promptly protested the Bowden run because his car was "over the weight limit." In perhaps the first example of international racing diplomacy, race officials salvaged American, German and British feelings by crediting *both* Bowden and MacDonald with an "official" speed record, in each of two classes.

Frank Crocker, a wealthy New Yorker, sped down the beach at 100 mph and swerved into the surf to avoid a bicyclist. Crocker and his French mechanic died in the crash.

As the millionaire sportsmen began to shy away from the driving duties—perhaps because of the Crocker crash, maybe due to rising horsepower and speed, or simply a matter of coincidence—the professional race driver came into being in 1906. However, he did not gain first class citizenship immediately.

The first professional drivers were little more than hired hands. They drove their bosses around and, generally, completed any unsavory task that needed doing—including risking their necks racing their bosses' cars—and were relegated to using the back entrance to the posh Ormond Hotel where the wealthy race fans stayed. The Europeans made a clear distinction between themselves and their drivers by listing only the last names of their chauffeurs. Consequently many old records do not indicate a given name.

In particular, Hemery, a Frenchman, was notorious for his rude snobbery; he insulted the Italians, snubbed the British, called the Americans "mechanical peasants," and tried to destroy the only car that was faster than his powerful Darracq, which was powered by the first V-8 anybody in Ormond/Daytona had ever seen. It had overhead valves and hemi heads. Keep in mind, it was 1906.

Hemery's only rival for the speed record was a soft-spoken American, Fred Marriott, driving the Stanley Steamer. Sensing the potential of the steam car, Hemery pulled alongside the wood- and canvas-bodied steamer, positioning his open exhaust stacks so they pointed directly at the side of the American car. He revved his engine, blacking the side of the Stanley, but not igniting it as Hemery had hoped. Hemery was disqualified by race officials and fired by the Darracq company. Marriott went on to beat the entire European aggregation by completing the world's first two-mile-per-minute run, setting a record of 127 miles per hour.

The sand was rough for the 1907 meet and drivers waited impatiently for tides to improve the surface. On the final day, Marriott rolled out the steamer and announced that he would make his run despite the rough conditions. "We'll glide right over the rough spots," he proclaimed. The boiler of the Stanley was wrapped with more than one mile of piano string to keep it from exploding under the stress of more than 1,000 pounds pressure.

The car was at maximum power as it streaked off the starting line with a blazing acceleration that only steam cars had in those days. He took nine miles to build up to the measured mile, and was doing an estimated 197 miles per hour as he reached the traps—he still was accelerating when he hit the rough part of the beach.

The streamlined racer took off, flying directly for the surf. It crashed in a thundering heap one-quarter of a mile from where it had left the sand, strewing parts everywhere. Marriott escaped serious injury, but the accident so shook the Stanley brothers that they gave up all future racing activities, which was a real setback to automobile racing history. Many automobile historians feel that had it not been for the crash, the Stanley brothers surely would have continued development of powerful passenger cars, and there is a possibility that we all might be driving steam cars today instead of gasoline-powered machines. It's an interesting thought, particularly to the oil companies—worldwide.

It took a 1,300 cubic inch-engined German car and three years to wrest the overall speed title away from the Stanley Steamer, but there was an American at the wheel when it happened—Goodyear's old friend, Barney Oldfield, who entered the Blitzen Benz and easily raised the record to 131.72 mph.

Proving himself more of a race driver than a prophet, he proudly proclaimed: "A speed of 131 miles an hour is as near to the absolute limit of speed as humanity will ever travel." Oldfield had all of the confidence characteristic of every racer to follow—and after all, it was 1910.

Continued from page 22

on his face. Mears returned the sinister smile. They were looking straight into each other's eyes, and only the two of them were able to share this special racing moment.

Barney Oldfield, left, in the famous Blitzen Benz in 1910; and above in 1912, with his ever-present cigar as he stands beside a homemade Land Speed Record car, awaiting an attempt at the record at Daytona Beach.

Every major race in the U.S. in 1919 was won on Goodyears, including the Indianapolis 500

In 1909, the center of American automobile production was not in Detroit, but Indianapolis, Indiana. The Hoosier capital boasted of more than one hundred manufacturers, some of them the finest names on the world's highways.

It was only natural, I suppose, that the greatest monument to speed ever built would wind up there. Carl Fisher and three other Indianapolis businessmen got together to build a race track on land owned by Fisher—so there was no question as to where it should be. *What* it was to be was mandated by several very simple factors. The track turned out to be a two and one-half mile oval for a very simple reason: that's all the land Fisher owned. The length of the race was set at 500 miles because of another elementary decree: that is all of the racing the cars could complete in daylight hours. The brick surface was used because asphaltum, which was the foundling stage of asphalt, didn't work. What was to become the absolute "Mecca" to race drivers and race fans from throughout the entire world began on very ordinary premises. But still it was a visionary accomplishment and Fisher's magnificent race track was often referred to as the Eighth Wonder of the World.

The first race held there was a somewhat informal affair—a shakedown—and shake it down they did. The surface of crushed stone and asphaltum broke up so badly that it caused the deaths of one driver, two riding mechanics and two spectators.

Fisher quickly made the decision to repave the oval with brick, which was the finest material available at the time and one of the prime industries of the area. The monumental task of placing more than three million bricks, each weighing more than ten pounds, was completed in an unbelievable sixty-three days.

The following year also was pretty much of a trial period, with dozens of races ranging from ten to two hundred miles being run. Finally the stage was set in 1911 for the world's premier automotive spectacular, the inaugural Indianapolis 500.

The purse was an astronomical $25,000 and more than 80,000 fans showed up, which, even then, made it the largest single-day sporting event in the world.

The cars were an interesting blend of the finest Europe had to offer and the best of America—mostly Indiana cars. Nearly all of the cars were stripped-down versions of passenger machines. The race began at promptly ten in the morning, under cloudy skies and American Johnny Aitken immediately took the lead in his Indianapolis-built National, which he had purchased a few days before from the local plant. Spencer Wishart piloted his Mercedes to the lead, only to give way to Fred Belcher in a Knox.

On Lap Twelve, Arthur Greiner hit the wall, throwing his mechanic, Sam Dickson, from the car to his death. The most spectacular crash of the day came at about the half-way mark when Joe Jagersberger's Case broke a steering part and spun, throwing his riding mechanic to the track. Harry Knight swerved to the left to miss the injured mechanic who lay on the bricks and crashed into the pits, where he demolished Herb

Lytle's Apperson and Caleb Bragg's Fiat. Unbelievably there were no serious injuries in that crash.

The role of the riding mechanic was not only an important one but a courageous one. It was one thing to roar around the track in those crude machines; it was another to ride along while somebody else did it. But it was an important role because the mechanic was often needed, for repairs and to keep the driver informed as to his position and to who might be overtaking.

There was one car that did not have a riding mechanic. Ray Harroun had designed his roadster in such a sleek manner that there wasn't room for another body in the cockpit, so he did the next best thing, he invented the rear-vision mirror, a device that eventually showed up on almost every passenger car in the world. Harroun had started twenty-eighth in the forty-car field, but he streaked into the lead late in the race in his yellow Number 32 Marmon Wasp and second-place finisher Ralph Mulford in a white Lozier couldn't catch him.

Harroun had won the world's premier motorsports event, partly through ingenuity and the rest through skill and courage. He proved that he also had a certain amount of gray matter by proclaiming in Victory Lane, "I've conquered the grandest automobile race in the world, so what is left?" He announced his retirement from racing right on the spot. Few racers have used such good judgment since.

Goodyear executives read with piqued interest the accounts of the spectacular race. Perhaps it was time to enter their sensational "cord" tires. They pondered the situation and actually supplied tires for some of the cars in the 1913 race, with the Stutz of Charles Metz finishing third. Another Stutz, driven by Gil Anderson, was in contention to win the race until a broken camshaft forced it out of the fray on the 187th lap.

But it was not the Goodyear tires that attracted the most attention, it was the Goodyear "Balloon." Here's a newspaper account of the balloon's appearance as printed in *The Indianapolis News:*

"GOODYEAR" CENTER OF INTEREST

> The balloon "Goodyear" was the center of considerable attention at the Decoration Day auto races at Indianapolis. The balloon was sent...by the Aeronautical Department. Plans had been made to take passengers in the Car (gondola), but owing to the high winds this was not attempted and the balloon was sent up captive. A local balloon manufacturer had three balloons also on the grounds but all three burst from the wind pressure. The "Goodyear," however, passed through the ordeal without mishap and remained in the air for several hours.

The score, on balloons, at least: Goodyear 3, Other Guys 0. It would be four more years before actual blimps were made, but it points to Goodyear's interest in the air as well as on the ground.

European Entries Flood Indianapolis

The 1914 Indianapolis race was totally dominated by European drivers and cars, with the first four places going to the men and machines from France: René Thomas in a Delage, Arthur Duray in a Peugeot, Albert Guyot in a Delage and Jules Goux in a Peugeot. The highest placing American was, you guessed it, Barney Oldfield in a Stutz, an Ohioan in an Indiana car, as American as, say, Grant Wood. It could have been called the "American Gothic" racing team.

It goes without saying that it was not a good year for Goodyear, or Americans in general.

Goodyear motorcycle tires in 1914. The place and the people are unknown, but not the Wingfoot.

Goodyear took a guarded interest in the race until World War I interrupted the competition but, following the two-year hiatus caused by the "war to end all wars," Goodyear Cords went racing again, with a vengeance.

What exactly were racing tires in those days? Here's how a company brochure explained them:

> As far as materials and construction are concerned, the cord tires used in racing are no different from those used on passenger cars. There are, of course, some points of variance, owing to the terrific speed which they must withstand in the speedways but never encounter in anything like ordinary use.
>
> The main point of difference is the tread of the tire. Tires suitable for use on a board track are constructed with a thinner tread than regular automotive tires wear. On account of the terrific centrifugal force attained by a tire revolving 18 to 20 times a second, as in the case when a car travels at the rate of 120 miles an hour, the thick tread on a regular automobile tire would work loose from the carcass and be thrown from it.
>
> So racing tires have thin treads. And here a different problem has been worked out. This has been to devise a tread, not so thick as to render the tire too "lively" and yet thick enough to give satisfactory wear.
>
> Until the last two racing seasons drivers were generally committed to the clincher principle of holding the tire to the rim,

and held tenaciously to the belief that only clincher tires would stay on rims at the terrific speeds maintained in racing.

Ralph DePalma was the first of the well known racing drivers to break away from this tradition and his example (of using straight side tires) has been followed by a majority of the racing men. One of the advantages of the straight side tire has over the clincher, is that it is not as susceptible to tube pinching. Another advantage is that it is much easier to mount and dismount, for the tire slips right over the straight side rim, obviating the necessity of prying the bead into the hooked rim, as is required when clincher rims are used.

It is seldom that a tire "blows" on the race track. Tires on cars pulling into the pits for a change were more often changed because of tube pinches than for any other cause.

It is the duty of the mechanic riding with the driver to observe the wearing down of the tires in a race and get the car to the pits before a tire has a chance to blow.

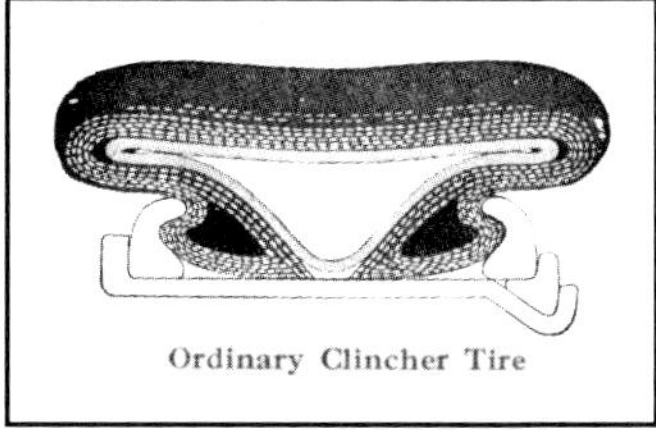

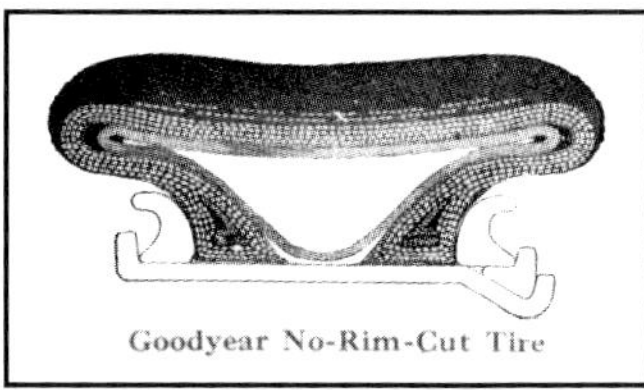

From a 1911 ad, comparison between ordinary clincher tire and Goodyear's No-Rim-Cut tire.

Left, a 1916 ad which appeared in National Geographic Magazine.

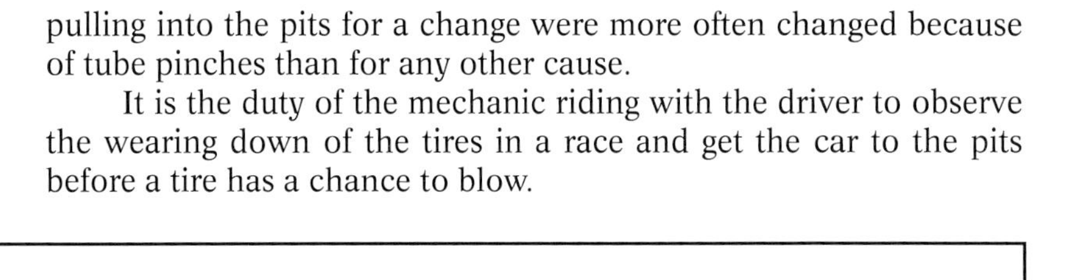

Motoring Masses Coming to Cords

TWO-THIRDS of all the new cars being equipped by the makers with cord tires are going out on Goodyear Cord Tires. But a growth even more striking than that is taking place.

Goodyear Cord Tires are standard equipment on the Franklin, the Packard Twin Six, the Locomobile, the Peerless, the White and the Haynes Twelve.

But you will also see them widely used now on cars like the Hudson, Stutz, Velie, Buick, Hupmobile, Chevrolet, Apperson, Dodge Brothers, Kissel, Oakland, Jackson, Oldsmobile, Chandler, Paige, and so on.

Simply because owners have learned that any good car gains in looks, in power-saving and gas-mileage, and in smooth riding, through Goodyear Cords.

Oversize, flexibility, and resiliency combine in these tires to produce real riding luxury by absorbing most of the jolt and jar of travel; to give unusual freedom from tire trouble; and to work economies by giving long service, and by saving power and fuel.

Their flexibility and resilience enable them to absorb road shocks without danger of stone-bruise and blow-out; add miles per gallon; assist in a quicker get-away; and make the car coast farther when power is shut off.

The oversize is very marked, and provides an increased cushion of air, which serves to emphasize the easy-riding and the other good qualities built into Goodyear Cord Tires.

The Goodyear Tire & Rubber Company
Akron, Ohio

Double-thick All-Weather and Ribbed Treads, for rear and front wheels. The deep, sharp All-Weather grips resist skidding and give great traction. The Ribbed Tread assists easy steering.

No-Hook and Q. D. Clincher types, for gasoline and electric cars.

Goodyear Tires, Tubes and Tire Saver Accessories are easy to get from Goodyear Service Station Dealers everywhere.

"Mention the Geographic—It identifies you."

Strategy and engineering were, even then, making great strides. The 150-lap race at Uniontown, Pennsylvania, on October 20, 1917 is a perfect example:

With only a few laps remaining, driver Eddie Hearne's car threw a tread, a common occurrence on a race track. On the next lap, Hearne stopped at his pits for a new tire, but the Goodyear man who was managing Hearne's pit that day, instead of changing the tire, gestured emphatically with a hammer for Hearne to get back in the race.

Hearne obeyed and won easily. He obviously didn't know what Goodyear knew; the tires would run from twenty-five to seventy-five miles on the track even after the tread was gone.

The first race of the 1919 season was won by Cliff Durant in a Chevrolet Special. It was at Santa Monica, California, on the 7.4-mile road course. He covered the 250 miles in three hours and four minutes at the blazing road course speed of more than eighty-one miles per hour. Non stop. The second place finisher was Hearne in the other Chevrolet Special. Also non stop. Both were on Goodyears.

They all but took over American racing—and some of Europe, dominating the sport so much that twenty-seven of the thirty-three cars entered in the 1919 Indianapolis 500 were shod with Goodyear Cords.

When the qualifying speeds for the first post-war race soared past the 100-mile-per-hour mark, even the race fans marveled at the "strength of the Goodyear tires."

René Thomas started from the pole, with Howdy Wilcox right beside him. Both men were driving blue cars, Thomas a Ballot and Wilcox a Peugeot, which was one of two cars that had been supplied by the Indianapolis Motor Speedway. Jules Goux, the 1913 winner, drove the other Speedway entry.

Wilcox drove a masterful race, not charging to the front, but staying within striking distance. At about the half-way point Wilcox passed Louis Chevrolet to take the lead, which he steadily increased. By the end of the race he was more than four minutes ahead of the second car, Eddie Hearne's Stutz.

The race was marred by the deaths of two drivers and one riding mechanic. For Goodyear, it was the greatest day in their early history. Wilcox had two tires go the entire 500 miles and the cars of Louis Chevrolet and Ira Vail, finishing eighth and ninth, covered the entire distance with no tire changes at all, which truly was a remarkable feat, particularly for 1919.

Goodyear was the toast of racing and no serious driver wanted to be without a set of the splendid "Cords."

The following front page story appeared in the June 1919 issue of the Goodyear Tire News:

GOODYEAR TIRES WIN AT INDIANAPOLIS RACES

> The great Five Hundred Mile Liberty Sweepstakes on May 31—the automobile racing classic of America—was a wonderful victory for Goodyear. Never did tires perform such wonderful service. Of the thirty-three starters, twenty-seven were on Goodyear Cords, and of the prize-winning cars nine were Goodyear shod.
>
> Wilcox, the winner, used only seven tires, two of his original equipment going the entire distance. Eddie Hearne, who took second money, also had two tires that lasted the entire route. Ira Vail, who came eighth, did not make a tire change.
>
> No service ever required of tires is greater than that of the

grueling grind of these racers over the brick-paved oval track at Indianapolis with its banked turns.

It makes the most astonishing story of tire performance in the history of the automobile.

One hundred thousand people packed the various grandstands and overflowed into the spacious oval. Around the entire course of 2-1/2 miles automobiles were parked against the track fence, in many places two and three deep.

Of all the race tracks in the country the Indianapolis course is the hardest on tires as the surface construction is of brick, which is more severe on tires than the board tracks of the various other speedways. So that the severe demand from tires in the big 500-mile race classic at Indianapolis is the most exacting that any racing tires are called upon to deliver anywhere. Yet the performance of Goodyear Cord tires and tubes in this biggest race of the year is the most astonishing feat that they have recorded since Goodyear began equipping racing cars with tires.

An array of 33 cars lined up for the start, in eight rows of four each, with the left over car bringing up the rear. An indication of how well Goodyear Cord tires are regarded by the big drivers of the speedways is found in the fact that 27 of the starting cars rolled past the judges stand on Goodyears. And that their faith was not unwarranted is indicated in the finish of 9 of these 10 cars within the money—on Goodyears.

And never was greater service demanded from tires than in this race. The day was terrifically hot [87-degrees F] and running tires over the hot, tile-like surface of the track was almost like holding them against an emery wheel.

The same story was told in newspapers across the country in an advertisement which carried a headline that read: "A PERFORMANCE THAT HAS NO PARALLEL."

Lessons Learned on the Race Track

Every major race in the United States that year was won on Goodyears and the legendary Ralph DePalma, driving a 905 cubic inch-engined Packard, broke every speed record from one to twenty miles on the smooth sand at Daytona Beach, reaching almost 150 miles per hour in one run.

DePalma used only one set of tires for nearly 700 miles of racing and practicing at Daytona. The very same set sped him to a world's record for a road course at Santa Monica, California, one month later.

Ralph DePalma at Daytona Beach, 1919.

SPECIAL RACING EDITION

GOODYEAR TIRE NEWS

VOL. 8. No. 6. AKRON, OHIO, U. S. A. JUNE, 1919

GOODYEAR TIRES WIN AT INDIANAPOLIS RACES

THE great Five Hundred Mile Liberty Sweepstakes at Indianapolis on May 31—the automobile racing classic of America—was a wonderful victory for Goodyear. Never did tires perform such wonderful service. Of the thirty-three starters, twenty-seven were on Goodyear Cords, and of the ten prize-winning cars nine were Goodyear shod.

Wilcox, the winner, used only seven tires, two of his original equipment going the entire distance. Eddie Hearne, who took second money, also had two tires that lasted the entire route. Ira Vail, who came eighth, did not make a tire change.

No service ever required of tires is greater than that of the gruelling grind of these racers over the brick-paved oval track at Indianapolis with its banked turns.

It makes the most astonishing story of tire performance in the history of the automobile.

Howard Wilcox *The Winner*

One set of Goodyears took Ira Vail the whole distance.

Eddie Hearne *2nd.*

Jules Goux *3rd.*

Ready for the Start

After a lapse of four years during the period of the war, automobile racing came back stronger than ever at the famous Indianapolis Speedway, in the big 500 mile event held there May 31—the first since Ralph De Palma's great victory in 1915. One hundred thousand people packed the various grandstands and overflowed into the spacious oval. Around the entire course of 2½ miles automobiles were parked against the track fence, in many places two and three deep.

Of all the race tracks in the country the Indianapolis course is the hardest on tires as the surface construction is of brick, which is more severe on tires than the board tracks of the various other speedways. So that the service demanded from tires in the big 500 mile classic at Indianapolis is the most exacting that any racing tires are called upon to deliver anywhere. Yet the performance of Goodyear Cord tires and tubes in this biggest race of the year was the most astonishing feat that they have recorded since Goodyear began equipping racing cars with tires some three years ago.

An array of 33 cars lined up for the start, in eight rows of four each, with the left over car bringing up the rear. An indication of how well Goodyear cord tires are regarded by the big drivers of the speedways is found in the fact that 27 of the starting cars rolled past the judges' stand on Goodyears. And that their faith was not unwarranted is indicated in the finish of 9 of these 10 cars within the money—on Goodyears.

And never was greater service demanded from tires than in this race. The day was terrifically hot and running tires over the hot, file-like surface of the track was almost like holding them against an emery wheel.

Ralph De Palma on his twenty-seventh lap, while making a stop for oil and water, changed three tires, and Wilcox a little later repeated this performance. Yet Wilcox used only seven tires in the race, and at its finish still was running on two tires that had completed the entire 500 miles.

The experience of Eddie Hearne was similar, as he also finished with two tires unscathed. Ira Vail, driving a Hudson, at the finish of his 500 miles was still driving on the same four tires with which he started the race, and the tires looked good for many more miles.

(Continued on Page 2)

The season went on, with most of the nation's leading drivers pledged to the Goodyear brigade—the Chevrolet brothers, Louis and Gaston; Tommy Milton in his Duesenberg, and Joe Boyer to name a few, raced on the famous tires.

Goodyear was so captivated at this point that the company printed and dedicated a booklet to "the drivers." In addition to thanking the "courageous young men who drive the racing cars," the book spelled out the company's philosophy:

> Man always has been interested in contests of speed, stamina and endurance.
>
> The feats of the gladiators and athletes of old are brought down to us in history; the knightly tournaments of the Middle Ages fill pages and volumes of the literature of that time; and one needs but to turn to the daily newspaper to appreciate the weight and importance given to the sporting events of today.
>
> History abundantly proves that contests of strength, skill and hazard not only improve the individual but that whole nations and peoples have been thus benefited, as is attested by the almost super

manhood of ancient Greece and Rome, no small part of which was directly attributable to a universal participation in sports and contests of all kinds.

As man found that the spirit of contest tended to improve the human race, he turned his attention to the improvement of his animal servants by the same means. Horse racing, therefore, has been for centuries a popular sport in many countries, for the reason that it tended to improve the breed of the horse, the faithful animal on which man depended so largely both in an industrial and a military way for so many years. Horse racing was encouraged in the early days by the governments of nearly all of the leading nations of the world for that reason. It was called the "Sport of Kings" because it came to be the pastime most popular among the nobility, and because it received the encouragement of the State.

With the advance of time the usefulness of the horse has been supplemented by automotive power.

The motor is the ascendancy, and it is to the purring internal-combustion engine that man looks today to his principal ally with which to fight the battle of life. It has become at once his time and money-saver during working hours and his main source of recreation in his spare time.

Everybody is interested in the development of the motor car. Yet most of us have taken as a matter of course the remarkable strides that have marked the improvement from the one-cylinder contrivance of only two decades ago to the long, low, rakish and comfortable high-powered car of today.

A large part of this development must be credited to lessons learned on the automotive speedways.

Just as in the past the horse race and the purses hung up for the victors spurred on the horse breeder to prize strains noted for speed and endurance, so has the automobile race with its promise of riches and fame to winners urged the racing drivers to seek and find more speed, power and ease of handling.

And behind these men of the speedways has been the manufacturer, on guard against defects, alert for improvements that would bring his car to as near perfection as might be attained.

At one and the same time the automobile race satisfies the human desire for tests of speed and endurance while bringing about a steady improvement of the automobile.

Hundreds of thousands of people attend the automobile races and enjoy the thrills of the speedway. To those of the hundreds of thousands who have studied the sport it is apparent that these races have a deeper and more important significance than appears on the surface. It is from the lessons learned on the race track that manufacturers have been enabled to improve their production of cars. The engines, the accessory parts, and the tires, all have been improved through lessons the track has taught.

The message went out in 1919. *Nobody ever said it better*. In fact, it could be mailed out, unchanged, today.

CHAPTER THREE

The clouds of racing emerged from the winds of another war

It not only was a great period for Goodyear, but perhaps the beginning of racing public relations and advertising copy that would continue to embellish not only tires but a host of other automotive products until today, when it has become commonplace. In 1919, it was unique. But Goodyear, knowing full well the feat they had accomplished, couldn't resist reminding the general public of their slogan, "More people ride on Goodyear Tires than on any other kind." Racing might have been the reason, but many within the company had begun to take a long, hard look at motorsports involvement.

In a letter dated March 4, 1921, C.C. Parther, who was manager of Products Division, Service Department, an attempt was made to continue Goodyear's racing effort. It was written to G.M. Stadeleman, chairman of the Operating Committee. The subject was the International 500-Mile Automobile Race, May 30, 1921:

This ad from March 6, 1920 illustrates the company's use of its success in automobile racing to enhance passenger tire sales.

At the Indianapolis car race last May and the Uniontown race last June and the Tacoma race in July we were afforded an opportunity. Oldfield, with practically no experimental work placed his own tire in the field and it excelled ours in both tread union and tread wear. Goodyear heavy tread tires would not wear [at] Indianapolis on the brick speedway and it was beyond the question of using them on the board speedway because the tread would not hold up.

Our light tread tires had fairly good tread union [the splice] but were inferior to Oldfield's in spite of the fact that he was using heavy tread tires. In cases where our tread stayed on, we could not expect more than 200 miles from the light treads on the board speedways. The development immediately started working on a black, non-blooming stock which worked well from the beginning. The first time it was used was last spring at Elgin by DePalma, who won the 300 mile race without a stop. The wearing quality of the tread was encouraging because it was better than the tire Oldfield had developed. The same tire was taken to the next race on the board speedway at Uniontown and proved to be superior to anything tried.

We then made light tires using the same compound, making slight changes in friction, and using very loosely woven barrier fabric. The next race was Fresno in which the tires proved superior to Oldfield's in every respect, though we encountered some problems in throwing treads. This information was given to the development department and more changes were made.

The Thanksgiving race at Los Angeles found us with only two drivers willing to use Goodyear tires. In this event [Roscoe] Saries and [Eddie] Miller finished the race in first and second without a stop.

Since we had only two cars equipped with Goodyear we would not like to draw the conclusion that the tires were satisfactory. On Washington's Birthday in Los Angeles, the tires on [Ralph] DePalma's, Saries' and Miller's cars repeated the performance.

Benefit to the general line: This tread has never been used before and when its wearing qualities became apparent, some pneumatic truck tires were built, which proved extremely satisfactory. Just as soon as these tires have been run long enough to prove the merits of this compound, some tests should be made on our passenger tires.

Why we should continue to race: We feel we should continue to race on a small scale for two good reasons: The next race at Indianapolis will be 500 miles on the brick speedway. We feel that we should take advantage of the opportunity of giving this tread the most severe test at that time. As much can be accomplished along this line in a few hours as can be accomplished through road tests in several months. Again we feel that some consideration should be given to the drivers who have been loyal to us when our tires were inferior to others. We know that DePalma, Saries, Miller, [Jules] Goux, and many others are looking to Goodyear for tires in the future. Recently Jimmy Murphy has asserted himself very strongly that he wants to ride on Goodyear. DePalma, Goodyear's best friend as a racing driver, is equipping his car to go the entire 500 miles without a stop. He is depending on Goodyear tires to make this run.

In view of the foregoing we would like permission to build fifteen 32 X 4.50 and twenty-five 33 X 5 heavy tread tires of the new construction to equip DePalma's, Saries', Murphy's and two other cars.

We feel that we can hardly leave some of these drivers to the mercy of Oldfield, who will be at Indianapolis with a number of tires that will doubtless be very arbitrate.

The latest cost of the 32 X 4.5 heavy tread tire is $36 and of the 33 X 5 will be $40. Fifteen of the former and twenty-five of the latter will cost us $1,500.

The other alternative would be to charge the drivers, which would be about ten percent above cost and offer prize money, possibly to the extent of $5,000.

I would appreciate having this considered by the Operating Committee as early as possible.

Yours,
C.C. Parther

It was a noble and obviously viable effort, but in 1921, the nation faced an economic depression and Goodyear began a reorganization. It was belt-tightening time. The company's founder, Frank A. Seiberling, resigned to form yet another company, the Seiberling Tire and Rubber Company. E.G. Wilmer and P.W. Litchfield took over the reins of Goodyear. They and the rest of the board members began to take a hard look at the racing expenditure. Besides, they rationalized, they had proved the technological leadership of their cord racing tires. They stunned the entire racing world by dropping out of active participation in the sport in 1922, saying that there was "nothing left to prove," in automotive competition.

This left Firestone, which had put tires on Ray Harroun's 1911 winning car, virtually alone in the United States as a developer and builder of racing tires. They had inherited a place in the sun, a spot which they were to hold onto for decades to come.

The demand for more comfort from automobiles led tire companies to look for ways to cushion the ride with lower profile, smaller diameter tires and wheels, resulting in so-called balloon tires—big, by comparison doughnut-looking tires.

Goodyear produced them for passenger cars, Firestone took them to the race track. In 1925, Peter DePaolo rolled his Duesenberg into victory lane at Indianapolis on Firestone balloon tires, becoming the first man to complete the 500 miles at an average speed in excess of 100 miles per hour. He received not only the fame and fortune for winning the race, but a special bonus from Firestone for using the company's new balloon tires.

Many sighs and lingering looks to the past were exhibited at Goodyear headquarters.

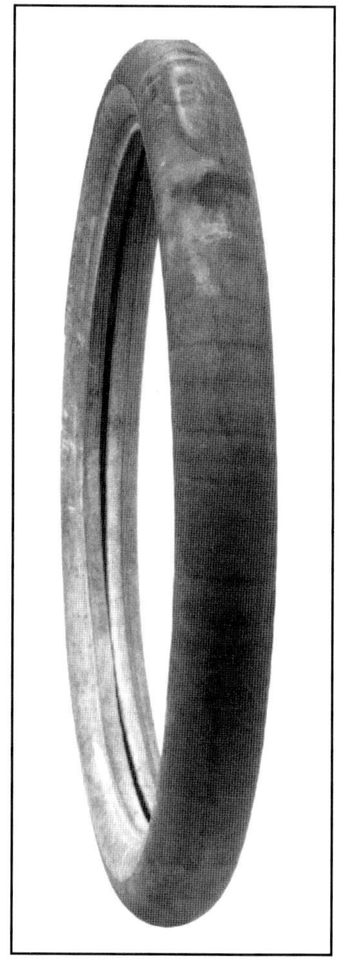

The tire directly above is a standard narrow tire of the period. To the right is Goodyear's new balloon tire—note difference in width.

The 1928 Chevrolet, above left, sports the new balloon tires with Goodyear's popular diamond-pattern All-Weather tread.

Note the size of the promotional tire on display in Tucson in the early Thirties.
Arizona Historical Society, B34307

But the Wingfoot Kept on Racing

Regardless of any executive decision to abstain from racing, there still were some Goodyears finding their way to race tracks and to another form of high speed adventure.

In the late 1930s and early 1940s, a new form of racing was blossoming—stock cars on little old dirt tracks, particularly throughout

the Southeast. Dirt race tracks had begun to spring up everywhere, small towns and large.

There is a band of red clay that starts up around Richmond, Virginia, and it runs down through Alabama and Georgia, right through Atlanta. So all a guy had to do in those areas was go out into any field and cut a quarter- or a half-mile track and wet it down with fifty thousand gallons of water and he had a race track.

Red clay is the greatest natural racing surface in the world; it will bond with anything. But white clay, found mostly in South Carolina, won't bond with anything. It gets super hard and makes big holes in the track. So the drivers had two distinct racing surfaces.

It was on these two types of tracks in the South that stock car racing was well on its way to becoming a regional pastime. And Goodyear tires were there. The company didn't supply them, the dealers didn't recommend them, but they were on a lot of the cars, nonetheless. The drivers had good luck with them on their highway machines, so a lot of them raced on them. It was as good a reason as any, because there weren't any stock car racing tires available, so what worked on the street would work on the track. It only stood to reason.

Keep in mind, these were pretty much pure stock cars, mostly Ford coupes, with the mufflers off so they would sound fierce, and some stiff springs and shocks. On a quarter-mile track, they didn't get much past sixty or seventy miles per hour, but with some work on the engines, they did it quickly. The fact is, the whole affair was somewhat like a fist fight on wheels.

What these pioneer drivers lacked in skill, they made up in bravado and plain old nerve. They banged on each other and usually the one who won was the one who banged the hardest or was able to stay out of a relative amount of trouble. There was little dexterity involved, just an ability to manhandle a car and the intestinal fortitude to carry it out.

The cars were stock in virtually every aspect—headlights, horns, fenders and tires. Many drove their cars to the track, put tape over the headlights to prevent breakage from flying rocks, and they simply lined-up and raced for a checkered flag. And then they drove them home and probably to work the next day, providing, of course, there was enough left of them.

Sometimes, there was a twenty-dollar bill for the winner, usually there was a cheer from the crowd and a slap on the back. Nothing more. But that was pay enough because vanity has always been one of the race driver's strongest suits.

One theory is that this southern concept of racing stemmed from the illegal running of homemade liquor—moonshine—from mountain stills to city customers. Drivers developed tremendous skills in high-speed runs on twisting two-lane blacktop mountain roads, followed by lawmen in hot pursuit. With the skills came the bragging about who could drive the best—and it was back to the country horse racing tracks to prove the point.

The shine runners—"wheelmen," they were called—obviously had the best chance of winning races because they not only had high-speed experience, they had hot cars, usually modified to the hilt.

One driver who limited his "racing" to the highway at night was Otis Walker. He was considered by all who knew anything about moonshine, to be the best of the wheelmen. His car was lightning fast and he, like many of his counterparts, ran on stock Goodyear tires. "They work the best in tight spots," he often said. And he was in many "tight spots."

"Otis would let you pull right up beside him," says Willard Fansler, a retired probation officer who lives on a mountainside in Basye, Virginia, a stone's throw from the present moonshine country. "Now don't get me wrong; you had to work your ass off to *get* there, because he was always going like the hammers of hell. But he'd wait till you got right up beside him—and you were usually going as fast as you could go—and he'd look over at you and grin. And that's the last you ever saw of him. He'd do it every time. Nobody ever knew what he had under that hood.

"I was chasin' him one night and stayin' up with him pretty well, and I had already figured on just runnin' him until he broke, because he was really loaded with shine—the springs were really saggin'—and I figured that if I chased him long enough, he would blow a supercharger or something. But all of a sudden, we came up on this running block. You know what a running block is?" he asked.

Without waiting for an answer, he explained: "A running block is where they get four cars out on the road, two in front of you and two behind you, and they just block you in and keep slowin' down until they get you stopped. That's a running block.

"Well, we came up on the two cars in front—they were state troopers," recalls the old-time Fed. "They were doin' about ninety. They didn't know who I was because my car was unmarked; in fact, it was a '40 Ford coupe, just like Otis's, and souped-up almost as much. I looked in the rear-view mirror, and here came the other two cars up behind us. I guess they figured we were both runnin' whiskey.

"I thought, 'I don't want Otis to get caught this way.' I had built up a respect for the man and I wanted to be the one who caught him. If it wasn't me, I wanted it to be a fair chase. This block sure wasn't.

"I didn't any more than get the thought out of my mind when I saw these two balls of smoke come from behind Otis's rear Goodyears, and I knew what he had done. He had caught second gear, and he was heading right for the front two cars. He hit the one on the right first, on the left rear quarter panel, and then he hit the one on the left in the right rear panel.

"They had been driving about four feet apart, so as to use up all the road," says the retired Fed, who is about as excited and animated as he must have been that night in the Forties on the lonely Carolina back road. "When Otis hit them, one car went in the ditch on one side of the road and the other went in the other ditch. It was like a perfect two-cushion billiard shot. And it was the damnedest piece of driving I ever saw. The two cars behind stopped to see if their fellow officers were all right. They were, I found out later. Only their pride was hurt.

"I figured right then if a man's good enough to do that, damn if I'll run him till he's crippled. So when he put it into a broad slide and skidded off to a side road a little way up, I stayed right on the main highway. I slowed down and about ten miles down the highway the two highway patrol cars that had been in the back caught me. I stopped and showed them my badge and said, 'I was chasin' him, too, but I'll be damned if he didn't get clean away.' "

They were a lot like World War I fighter pilots because there was a respect between men like Otis Walker and Willard Fansler. If the wheelman's springs weren't sagging, they knew he was empty and they didn't chase him. It was a mark of honor, much the same as many fighter pilots had refused to shoot down a plane in which they had been in a dogfight if the opponent was out of ammunition.

"I saw Otis the next day," says Fansler. "He wasn't carrying any shine, so he stopped and said, 'I really 'preciated that, Willard. You was givin' me a good chase. You know, when I slid in that side road, every one of them Goodyears was cryin' a different tune.' "

Otis Walker might have made it to the race track someday, but he died one Carolina moonlit night when the front end of the drive shaft on the Cadillac he was driving broke loose and dug into the asphalt, catapulting the car and Otis into history.

Goodyear never tried to capitalize on any of the daring nighttime exploits, for obvious reasons, but it had to give some of the executives who remembered the glorious days of Indianapolis some satisfaction in knowing that the best wheelmen out there were running their tires, although the company never said so. In print, at least.

Despite the winds of another war, the clouds of racing were building in the Southeast. But it would be another decade before Goodyear would do anything about it. Although they kept their eyes cast south, and watched.

After the War, Racing Grew Like an Octopus

Racing went off in many directions following World War II. One of the major events began in 1947 at an abandoned Navy airfield in Davie, Florida. Mal Carlisle promoted a winter racing season on the airfield, which was unique because, from the air, it looked like a wagon wheel. The runways were spokes and the rim was a two-mile-circle taxiway. It was an awesome sight and Carlisle knew it would be more than awesome with race cars blasting around it.

Many early stock car modified drivers who would later become famous drove in the first race: Buck Baker, Ralph Moody, Fonty and Tim Flock and Red Byron, to name a few. They ran their pre-war Ford coupes flat out on the big circle, using the tallest gears they could find. The speeds rose to more than 150 miles per hour, which easily surpassed the fastest Indianapolis qualifying time of that year, 128.755 set by Wild Bill Holland. This was the fastest race track in the world at the time. The cars ran on what appeared to be stock car tires—some of them Goodyear—but the Indy drivers who came to Davie obviously brought along some Indy Firestones.

Then Carlisle and Fred Gamble, who was later to come to Goodyear, concocted a one-eighth-mile circular track for midgets. The

Tire of tires: this is the Goodyear Double Eagle. Built to be better than is customarily needed; for those favored folk who can afford to forget they *have* tires on their cars. Something much more than a heavy duty tire—a *luxury* tire. So troubleproof and durable that under anything like normal conditions you can expect the Double Eagle to last as long as you will keep your car.

GOODYEAR

Double Eagle

1936 advertisement

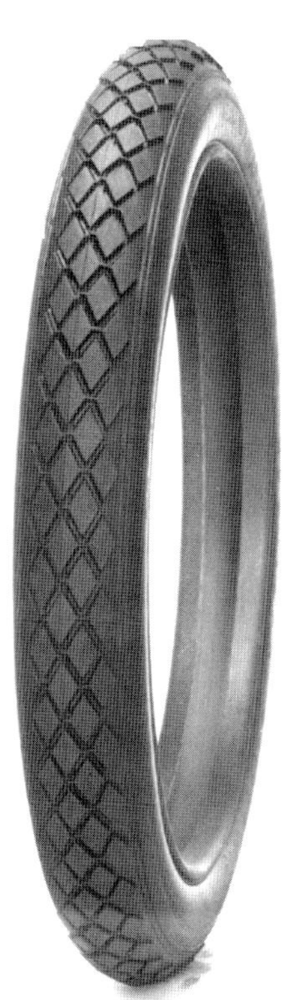

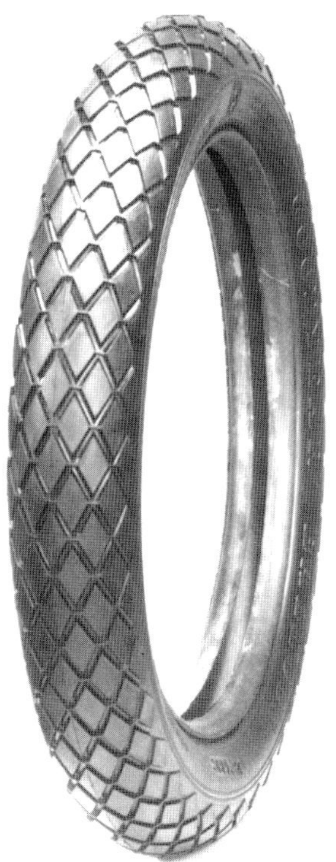

Goodyear had a variety of tires to choose from in the late 1920s.

From left to right, are; top: Clincher, all weather tread, 1925; Motorcycle balloon clincher, all weather tread, 1925; and Balloon motorcycle, 1927;bottom: All weather tire, 1928; Cord tire, narrow opening, 1928; Progress tire, wide opening, 1928; and a Speedway tire, 1928.

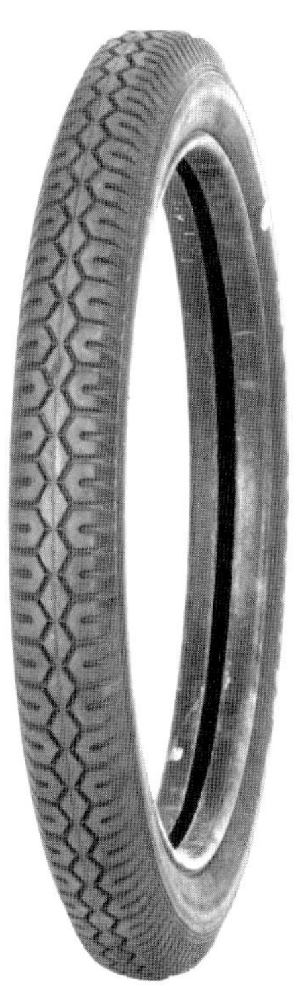

Above, left to right, are two more Speedway tires, 1928—note differences in the three tread patterns; and Goodyear's famous Double Eagle, 1929. To the right is a cutaway showing construction of the milestone-setting Double Eagle tire.

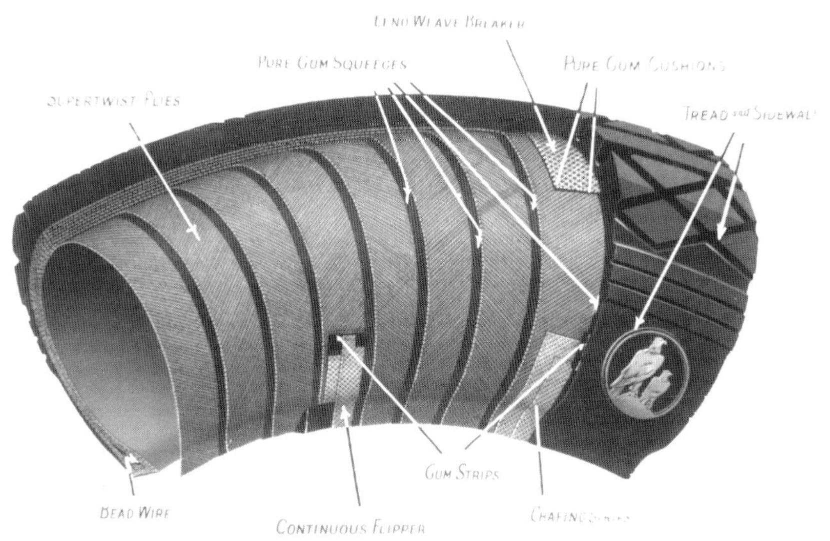

fans, who could see well enough to tell if the driver had shaved or not that day, loved it.

Not satisfied with running on the tiny track, which had been fashioned from a parking ramp, the midget drivers took to the big, two-mile circle, but were slightly slower due to gearing limitations. "The gears the stock car guys were using were bigger than the midget *cars*," Fonty Flock recalled. But even at that they turned laps at about fifteen miles an hour faster than their big-brother cars had done at Indy in 1947.

It was at this point that the American Automobile Association, which sponsored the Indy 500, stepped in and asked them not to run any more because it was "downgrading the Indianapolis 500."

On hand for the Davie races was a man who would have the greatest influence upon the sport of automobile racing of any who ever lived, William Henry Getty France. "Big Bill" France, who had successfully and spectacularly promoted stock car races at Daytona Beach, took note of what was happening. Although there's no record or recollection of his ever having said so, France must have filed away in his mind what a giant speedway for stock cars would be like in the South. It became obvious a decade later.

Stock car racing spread splashes of color and excitement to an otherwise dull and lifeless South.

For so many years the South was dull, a sepia-tone scenario. It seemed that there wasn't any spirit after the War Between the States; and don't think that because the war had been over for ninety years things had changed all that much. It was worse in some places: Charleston, for example, was still *fighting* the war.

Life in most parts of the South was gray and drab, sort of like a black-and-white movie, with nothing but cotton mills and farms and hard work. But that was starting to change in the 1950s, and stock car racing—the sport that was once frowned upon as a low-life affair—was part of the reason for the change. Colorful, fun-loving characters like Curtis Turner and Little Joe Weatherly were spreading splashes of Technicolor throughout the entire South, and the fans were eating it up. It was a traveling circus, going from small track to small track and leaving each a small hope. And a lot of pleasure.

Hard-driving Curtis Turner was one of NASCAR's all-time favorites.

While all of this excitement was going on south of the Mason-Dixon line Goodyear executives were casting an eye in that direction. It seemed that anything used on one of those race cars could be a rolling billboard to some, but still there was a great deal of resistance to jump in the fray as they had done in the early part of the century.

They continued to watch with an advertising and public relations view as well as an economic one. It would cost a lot of money to develop a racing tire again. So much had changed since the days of the clincher tires and riding mechanics of Goodyear's Indy domination.

For one thing, Firestone had the market to itself. Oh, they weren't working much on the stock cars—they seemed to have their hands full at Indianapolis, an arena that had proven to be the "best in the world." This upstart southern stock car craze had yet to prove that it was little more than a bunch of rough and tumble desperadoes, banging fenders and fighting a lot. Without doubt, stock car racing lacked the *panache* of the Indianapolis 500.

But it was growing, and when a big, asphalt superspeedway opened in Darlington, South Carolina, in 1950, a lot of race fans paid attention. As it turned out, it was probably the catalyst that got Goodyear off top dead center.

On Labor Day in 1950, a young organization with the cumbersome name of the National Association for Stock Car Auto Racing (NASCAR) announced that seventy-five cars would start the first Southern 500. It was to be the "Indianapolis of the South." More eyes turned in that direction. Was this the beginning of some organization from the chaos in which stock car racing had been mired for years?

With Bill France running things, most agreed that it was. "There must have been 30,000 people there on race day," recalled the late Bill Tuthill, who was one of NASCAR's organizers. "But we got down there early. In fact, the real story began before we got there. Bill France, Curtis Turner and Alvin Hawkins bought a new Plymouth sedan in Winston-Salem on the way to Darlington. They just wanted something to run around in while they were there and then they later planned to race it on a short track somewhere.

"It was always parked outside the Darlington Motel, and any time anybody needed to go after food or drinks or whatever, they took the little black Plymouth. We took it back and forth to the Elk's Club in Florence. Everywhere. We called it the 'taxi.'

"Well, Johnny Mantz," Tuthill continued, "was a hot-shot Indy driver and he had come down to find a ride for the Southern 500. But, the day before the race, he hadn't found one, so he came back to the motel, looking for the Plymouth."

"Where's the taxi?" he asked.

"I think somebody took it into town," Tuthill answered.

"Well, tell them to leave it here when they get back. I'm gonna' race it tomorrow."

"We weren't the only ones who thought he was crazy," said Tuthill. "Everybody did. Especially on race day. There were Oldsmobiles and Lincolns and Fords and Cadillacs, all with big V-8s. And here was Mantz in that six-cylinder Plymouth."

The Plymouth "taxi" that Johnny Mantz drove to victory in the first Southern 500 at Darlington.

But Mantz had one big advantage. He had come to Darlington with a set of Firestone Indy tires and he was the only one in the race with anything that even remotely resembled racing tires. Even though the Plymouth was heavier than an Indy car, the tires were built for speed.

That part didn't faze the other hot shoes. They were using Goodyear and Armstrong and Goodrich, whatever they thought would do the best job—but those were all street tires.

Mantz intended to put on a show, and that he did. He drove around the track, way up high, at a steady pace all day—about seventy-five miles an hour—and he did everything right. He pitted under caution, which was something that hadn't occurred to the other guys because they were used to short races. Mantz had Indy experience, where pitting was necessary. Generally, he made everybody else on the track as mad as hell. Particularly after he got into the lead.

Red Byron in Red Vogt's Cadillac and Fireball Roberts in an Olds 88 would blaze right by him, and then KERBOOM! a tire would blow and into the pits they would go. And there would be Mantz, tooling along, right through the banked turns and down the straightaway, right past the pits where everybody was frantically changing tires.

Turner said after the race that he knew with certainty how many pit stops he had made: "Twenty-seven, because I counted the blown-out tires in my pit."

Red Byron was a top beach course racer, copping four consecutive victories at Daytona between 1946 and 1949.

When the checkered flag was waved, Mantz was two laps ahead of the field. He had averaged 74 miles per hour. The fans cheered, although some were disappointed because they felt a little cheated that a sickly little Plymouth had out-distanced their favorite V-8 passenger cars—because these were *strictly* stock cars, just like they drove themselves. (Incidentally, this same tactic was used to win the first Indy 500 in 1911—and with the same average speed!).

Everybody in the pits was in a state of shock. Especially Red Vogt. He was over at the garage when the car was being inspected and he kept saying, "There's no damn way a Plymouth can beat a Cadillac. No way."

Vogt filed a protest, which meant the car had to be torn down. NASCAR officials spent the night at it, with Vogt looking over their shoulders, muttering "No way..."

When the sun rose, it was announced that the car was perfectly legal and Vogt stomped away, still muttering his strong sentiments and kicking at rocks in the dirt. If nothing else, this proved to drivers and crews that strategy was all important in a long-distance race. Not to mention tires.

CHAPTER FOUR

Daytona and Bill France

The inevitable postrace traffic jam—some things really don't change much! Eight miles of cars, four abreast, head home after a late Thirties beach race at Daytona.

Bill France, race driver and NASCAR founder, in his Blitzkreig Special which he drove in numerous races in the late Thirties.

Daytona Beach, which had been the World Capital of Speed since 1902, played more of a role in the organization of stock car racing than any other place; although it was one man, Bill France, who put together all of the pieces.

France and his family had taken up roots there in 1936, while on his way to Miami from their home in Washington, DC. One of the reasons the young race driver/mechanic had decided to stop in Daytona was the 1936 beach race that was planned. The purse was $100 and that was reason enough in those days.

The big man drove a 1935 Ford coupe, owned by a fellow mechanic named Glen Brooks. Ucal Cunningham, a Daytona gasoline distributor, sponsored France with fuel and Goodyear passenger car tires from his warehouse stock.

There surely were many other cars in the race on Goodyears but records don't indicate which car used what. The only thing they know is that the tires were all stock, so one can assume almost every brand available was used.

The City of Daytona had posted some big money for European racers to come over and race on the beach, going all the way back to 1902. It had been good for business, but with the Depression still very much at hand, they needed something that cost a lot less and might still draw tourists to their wide and beautiful beaches. Stock car racing might just be the ticket.

Sig Haughdahl, a local and the man who first had run three miles per minute on the beach in Land Speed Record runs, helped layout the course which would some day affect the future of auto and motorcycle racing in America, as well as keep the city in the spotlight it had occupied since the turn-of-the-century. And shape the future of both Bill France and big time automobile racing. Big time.

The course went down the beach highway a mile and a half, made a turn in the sand and came back up the beach to a north turn, which was just below where the measured mile had clocked the world's fastest cars for three decades. It was 3.2 miles around. With a course like that, stock passenger tires were close to being adequate. The race attracted many of the biggest names in the country. Among the entries were Indianapolis 500 winner Bill Cummings; dirt track champions Bob Sall, Doc MacKenzie and Ben Shaw; midget racing champion Bill Schindler; international racing star Major Goldie Gardner; the Collier brothers, Sam and Miles, two wealthy young sportsmen who—together with aviation entrepreneur Alec Ulmann—brought sports car racing to the front in America, and Palm Beach millionaire Jack Rutherfurd, who was famous for his exploits in both cars and boats. And Bill France.

France not only entered his '35 Ford but he served as mechanic on another Ford driven by Milt Marion, which was the first stock car to have national sponsorship from a company: Permatex.

National press coverage was extensive because of the quality of the field. As qualifying began, all could see that this combination beach/road course was going to present quite a show. Bill Cummings in a supercharged Auburn was the fastest qualifier in the twenty-seven car field at 70.39 miles per hour.

The cars started in reverse qualifying order, in an effort to give everybody an even chance, and to make the race more interesting for the fans. The cars also were given handicaps. The two slowest cars—both Willys—made three laps before the next car was turned loose.

"We didn't know until qualifying time if the beach was going to be rough or smooth," said France some years later. "We knew we would have to wait until the tide was half-way out before we could tell if it was decent to run on," he said. "There was no other way. Then we had to worry about the wind, because if it changed, it could affect how far out the tide would go and how fast it would come back in. We knew, for instance, that a strong east wind would bring a higher tide and not only affect the race but the thousands of passenger cars that had already parked near the grandstands at either end of the course. So everybody constantly checked the wind and the beach."

Fortunately the beach straightaway was smooth when the tide began to ebb, and the field blasted off about one hour before it was all the way out, giving them as much time as possible to run the one hundred and sixty laps the race committee had determined could be covered if Mother Nature cooperated.

"I started tenth, about eight minutes after the first car, but it didn't take me long to pass both Willys," said France. "Then, about fifteen minutes after that, Bill Cummings flew by me in the Auburn with the sand flying. I only saw him one more time in the race, and that was when he was in the pits," he recalled.

Cummings didn't last long. The Auburn was low and the sand apparently was scooped up under the hood and sucked into the supercharger. It took only sixteen laps to destroy the mighty engine. Rutherfurd, in the other Auburn, lasted twenty-six laps.

France, who had lived at the beach for a while, had an advantage. Being a racer, he had an understanding of the broad, sandy beach, and he knew how to "use it." He also knew that big, heavy cars, no matter how fast, weren't the answer. He felt it would be a Ford that would cross the finish line first.

Many of the race cars got in trouble late in the race because the turns had rutted out so much. Most of them got stuck at one time or

Curtis Turner thrills the crowd as he broadslides into the South Turn of the old Daytona beach course.

another. If they went too slowly, they mired down and had to be towed out. If they went too fast, they dug in and flipped, so it became a delicate trick to find just the right speed. A mile or so either way resulted in disaster of one sort or another.

Milt Marion was towed out five times, but, after each incident, he drove like crazy and caught up to whomever he thought was the leader of the race.

As if the confusion of the rutted course and tow trucks everywhere wasn't enough, the east wind did come up and the tide started back in much sooner than had been expected. There was a chance that hundreds of cars would be stranded on the beach after the race. So, when there was a big tangle in the North Turn that completely blocked the course at the 200-mile mark, the race was called and Milt Marion was declared the winner because they thought he was leading—although it was hard to tell with all of the confusion.

France recalled in later years that he thought they put Goodyears on Marion's car as well as his own, but he wasn't sure. It didn't matter much because the confusion that resulted erased any question of what was used on what.

The City Fathers took this opportunity to get out of racing. For one thing, they had lost $22,000 and the disarray made the whole affair a laughing stock throughout racing. But not to Bill France. He talked the local Elks Club into sponsoring the following year's race and then France went to the city council and told them that he and the Elks would like to take over promoting and running the race. They were more than pleased to hand over the reins to him.

The 1937 race was much more of a success because France and his makeshift crew added clay to the turns—"marl," as this particular type of clay is called in Florida. They waited until the final tide went out and then Volusia County bulldozers and steamrollers worked it in and smoothed it out. It was a great improvement over the 1936 course.

Smokey Purser, a local bar owner, won the race and collected his share of the purse, which was taken from the twenty-five-cent-per-person admission fee. He took home a whopping total of $43.56 for his great accomplishment.

The following year, Bill France not only became the promoter, but he won the race. He had raised the admission to fifty cents and the crowd was twice as large. The purse was larger, too. He won one hundred dollars.

The rest is history. France was, from this wild-and-woolly beach race, to eventually build the strongest racing organization the world has ever known.

Return to Racing

The lure of what was rapidly becoming the "great southern pastime" became too much for Goodyear to ignore; also the fact that the company's absence from racing had left rival Firestone as the only American company making specialized racing tires must have contributed to their new-found interest in the sport.

In the mid-1950s, Goodyear, looking for a way to overcome an overly conservative and stuffy image and to get ready to meet the maturing "baby boom" of the post-World War II era, decided upon a return to automobile racing.

The first test they conducted was at the Darlington Raceway in 1954, which, being the pinnacle of speed for stock cars, was the perfect place to start. Some of the car manufacturers had gone to Darlington with their cars for the new convertible series, which was a real crowd-pleaser because the fans could really see what was going on with the topless cars. It seemed like a perfect time for Goodyear to see what their

The crowds loved the convertible class started in 1954 because they could get better views of their favorite drivers. Here they race on the Daytona beach course, used from 1936 to 1959.

newly-designed stock car tires would do, so they showed up with some for the drivers to try. The tests were inconclusive because most of the drivers at that time weren't used to much more than highway tires, so they really couldn't tell the difference between a plain old stock tire and an improved racing tire. The basic reason was that the cars were stock and didn't handle all that well in the first place, even with improved tires. Conversely, it was difficult for Goodyear to design a true racing tire because they didn't have a real race car.

Those of lesser caliber would have thrown in the towel, but not Goodyear; it was another start-from-scratch situation. Almost nobody who had been at Goodyear in the Twenties when the company quit racing was around to foster the budding interest in the Fifties, but the spirit still was there. They took the simple Darlington tests as an indicator that their company was going to go after Firestone, tooth-and-nail. They began to formulate battle lines.

The idea to supply stock car tires actually had come from the original equipment sales people. They had worked closely with Chrysler Corporation because they were using Goodyear tires almost exclusively on their passenger cars.

Since Chrysler was starting to build some high performance cars, namely the 300, they felt the race track was the perfect place to showcase the vehicle. And they wanted to do it on Goodyears because those would be the tires on their street cars and the more "original" the equipment on

Lee Petty, left, was one of Goodyear's first tire-testers. Here he examines a 1958 racing tire.

the race car, the more their sales pitch would mean.

Stock cars still were pretty much that. They could use seat belts and roll bars, but that was about all. Still there was a little factory "tweaking" of the engines and suspensions and parts that could be made to look strictly stock but did, in fact, make them considerably more than "right from the showroom" vehicles. It was a behind-the-scenes battle of which few consumers were aware.

It wasn't the factories doing this, although there undoubtedly were some heads turned from time to time when parts orders went out; it was mostly the people who prepared the cars for racing who "adjusted" them to fit the situation. Carl Kiekhaefer was a prime example. He had built a strong reputation for powerful engines with his Mercury outboard boat motors, and had also made enough money in doing so that he could well afford to plow some of it into stock car racing.

Goodyear had taken its proven Police Special tire to the Darlington tests. The tire had been designed with a stronger carcass and a softer compound for better handling, and it was available only to legitimate police departments. It was, in its own way, a legend among tires of the Fifties, and although other tire companies claimed to have a tire "just as good," Goodyear pretty much controlled the law-enforcement market.

From this Police Special, Goodyear began a program that was the first step toward the "King of the Hill" sobriquet, a nickname many had wanted since the days long before when the company officially got out of automobile racing.

The police tires seemed to work well on the heavy Chryslers, so Kiekhaefer gave the okay for his people to start building two race cars, one each for Tim and Fonty Flock, who certainly were two of a handful of early drivers who had reached the "hero" plateau, at least, in the Southeast.

Kiekhaefer cars began winning on short tracks, and they won with such regularity that NASCAR officials became suspicious. Bill France

The Police Special was the base tire from which Goodyear started its postwar race tire development and racing program. This is the 1960 model.

The Kiekhaefer Chrysler 300s were among the first to race on Goodyear's police tires. Here Buck Baker is ready to race a Kiekhaefer car at Daytona.

Driver Tim Flock, left.

Land Speed Record tire developed by Goodyear in 1959 for Mickey Thompson; far left.

wanted to keep his newborn sport as pristine as possible, but he knew that a really good mechanic or suspension man could give a car an advantage that would be hard to detect. Officials checked and rechecked the Chryslers for irregularities but they never were able to find any.

They checked the fuel they were using. It was precisely the same Pure Oil gasoline that everybody else was running. The tires were offered by Goodyear as off-the-shelf items, although to a limited public. Besides, they were available to the other teams if they so chose, so there wasn't anything wrong there.

This suspicion that Kiekhaefer would stop at nothing to win followed him through all of his racing career, but no one was ever able to pin-point a single thing.

"The damn cars are just faster than anything else," he said smugly, "and if these guys want to be cry babies, let 'em go ahead. We'll beat 'em even more."

Most teams were so convinced that the Chryslers had been tampered with that they hardly noticed the Goodyear tires. Even though the modified Police Specials worked well, it was a relative thing. There was a lot of tire failure in every race. It was so commonplace that everybody expected it. Fewer of the Goodyears failed than did the assortment of other tires, but there was so much focus on Kiekhaefer engines that nobody paid much attention to the rubber. Few realized that it was the Goodyears that gave the Chryslers some of their advantage.

Kiekhaefer brought about some change in the rough-and-tumble sport of stock car racing. Up to that point, drivers raced in tee shirts—and sometimes no shirts at all—and the whole scene was one of grime and true grit. But Kiekhaefer was the first millionaire ever to come into NASCAR racing, at least that anybody knew about. Everybody certainly knew it about Kiekhaefer, though, because of the kind of show he put on; it was like somebody had booked Ringling Brothers & Barnum and Bailey. Nobody in racing ever saw anything like it. His team wore *uniforms*. The jeans and tee-shirt teams began to look like just that—"jeans and tee-shirt teams." Before Kiekhaefer, if teams dressed alike, no matter what it was, it was considered classy. And if a guy hauled a race car to the track on the back of a flatbed truck, everybody in the place talked about it, from the pits to the grandstands.

So when Kiekhaefer showed up at the races with not only a whole fleet of the hot new Chrysler 300s, but box vans to carry them in, it was the biggest thing that had happened in the history of stock car racing. They even had a separate box van for spare parts and equipment—everything from spark plugs to spare engines.

The entire crew for each car had identical uniforms—washed and starched for each race. Even his drivers had racing uniforms.

It was difficult to ignore the Kiekhaefer team. And Goodyear was fortunate to have been involved with them. It lent a certain air of credibility to their entire fledgling racing tire effort. The success with Kiekhaefer spurred Goodyear on. John Hartz, who was in charge of development, liked racing. He also was a favorite son of production vice president Russell DeYoung, who was soon to become president and later board chairman, so Hartz was given *carte blanche* to carry on. He gave the command to "go for it," and he chose a few good men to help carry out the task.

Gene McMannis was one of the men who began to look at various designs and compounds, and with little more than half a dozen associates working part-time on racing tires and the rest of the time on passenger tires, they started the arduous climb.

The complexities of building a fast, safe racing tire were so great that these chosen few began to work evenings and on weekends, because their regular duties of building good tires for the public became more and more demanding. More people *were* riding on Goodyear tires than on any other kind, and DeYoung and Hartz not only wanted to keep it that way but they wanted to widen the gap between themselves and "Number Two," Firestone.

Consequently there was only one way to improve the racing tire, and that was by working pretty much on their own time. The bottom line was "dedication," and that was without a doubt the single greatest factor, and remains so today, in Goodyear's phenomenal success.

It wasn't easy, and the climb to the top was fraught with many slides because there were few if any benchmarks. They began a design and development program for racing right from the grassroots. But that was nothing new for Goodyear. The company had been the pioneer in nearly every major advancement of tire design and production, so this new challenge was little more than that—a challenge. That's what the company thrived upon.

Dealers also were pressuring Akron to "do something." They were getting pretty tired of the Memorial Day massacre Firestone was subjecting them to each spring.

About the same time Mickey Thompson, a young California hot-rodder, began to take notice of the success of the Kiekhaefer cars. Thompson had his own dream. Long on ideas but short on funds, Thompson sold Pontiac Division of General Motors on supplying four engines for a new racing creation named *Challenger,* which would attempt to break Englishman John Cobb's World Land Speed Record of 396 miles per hour.

Four engines was not an unusual request because racers have always used up a lot of power plants, but the thing that made this vehicle different was the fact that Thompson intended to use all four of them simultaneously, one driving each wheel of the land speed record (LSR) streamlined vehicle.

Mickey Thompson closes the hatch prior to an attempt at the World's Land Speed Record in his Challenger I *at the Bonneville Salt Flats in 1959.*

Thompson immediately began looking for an innovative tire company that could build him some racing tires that would withstand the forces of speeds over four hundred miles per hour.

Thompson had designed the land speed car based around the four engines and insisted that the body and tires had to be no higher than the bulk of the Pontiac power plants.

Dunlop had dominated land speed racing up to that period with huge tires five feet or more in diameter. Bigger diameter meant less rolling speed with which the tire construction had to contend. Firestone apparently was of the same opinion because they had built some LSR tires and they were as large as the Dunlops had been.

Thompson came to Goodyear with his need for a tire no more than thirty inches in diameter. To exceed four hundred miles per hour. It was a stupendous request.

McMannis was the racing tire development engineer for Goodyear, with a young assistant by the name of Walt DeVinney. McMannis and DeVinney designed a radical new type tire for this project. It was a 700-21 with an overall diameter of thirty inches. This tire was extreme in the evolution of performance tires because it was the first ultra low profile tire anybody had ever seen. It had an aspect ratio of about sixty-four compared to conventional tires of the time that were in the eighties. Thus the Thompson tire became the grandfather of low profile tires.

Never before, in all its history, had Goodyear been asked to perform such an extraordinary task. Predictably, and with the same spirit with which they attacked each challenge, the engineers began to study the situation. What they came up with not only proved to be the answer to Thompson's tire dilemma, but also became the first step in revolutionizing the entire passenger car market.

What resulted was a tire of unique construction, one that was to become known as bias-belted and would sweep the consumer market in the late 1960s and early 1970s, paving the way for later acceptance of the radial tire.

The tire was constructed of plies running diagonally from bead to bead at an angle, one ply in one direction and the next in the opposite. The more plies, the stronger the tire construction. It was perhaps the strongest tire concocted up to that time.

Thompson made many attempts at the record on Utah's Bonneville Salt Flats but a combination of problems plagued his efforts. First he had difficulty coordinating the power of the four engines so that each delivered exactly the same thrust as the other. Then rough salt surface conditions caused the car to buck and bounce so badly that he couldn't hold it in a straight line. He got the car past the three-hundred-mile-per-hour mark, but never was able to surpass four hundred for a record, though he did hit 409 mph one-way.

The one problem Mickey Thompson didn't have was tires. They performed flawlessly.

The press began to wonder if Thompson really was serious about his attempt, so the determined hot-rodder rolled out the *Challenger* and said "Okay, guys, you drive it and see what you think of the salt conditions." He had no takers, but he proved a point. A disappointed Thompson went back to the drawing board.

NASCAR racing was a star to which Goodyear intended to hitch its wagon

This was stock car racing in the Fifties. The dust was often so bad that drivers simply followed the car in front of them.

There were signs of organization in NASCAR but still it was a rough sport. It would be several years before order was brought from this bedlam. Part of the problem was that many of the tracks still were dirt and that, in itself, was hard to regulate. But the fans loved it and this surely is where stock car racing got its start. At the dirt roots.

Dust was a problem in those early races, and it wasn't always as easy to overcome as sending somebody off to a corner with a flashlight. It was so bad one night in Oklahoma City that Lee Petty came down the straightaway, stopped his car, got out, and grabbed the red flag from the starter's rack and actually stopped the race himself.

And another time, it was so dusty that nobody could see a thing. Everybody was just following everybody else. Buck Baker was behind some guy who kept going slower and slower and slower. Finally he stopped completely and Buck ran into the back of him. Baker got out of his car and yelled:

"Why the hell did you stop?"

"Buck, I'm in the *pits*," the guy said as he surveyed the damage to his race car.

The driver had decided to hang it up and Buck had followed him right to his truck.

A lot of things happened to Buck. In one of those dusty races, he ran completely through the board fence one night, right out into the parking lot. He waited in his car and nobody came to check on him. He was as mad as a wet hen when he stomped back to the scoring stand.

"Why didn't nobody come and check on me?" he said. "I coulda' been hurt."

They all looked at each other in amazement.

"We didn't even know you were out of the race, Buck," one of them finally said.

It was obvious to Goodyear that stock car racing was well on its way to the top, in the Southeast, at least. It was a star to which they intended to hitch their wagon.

In January of 1957, the company decided to run some tire tests at a quarter-mile asphalt track in West Palm Beach, Florida. The design, compounding and development departments had all done their jobs. Additionally, they had come up with a name for their racing tire—the *Stock Car Special.*

And they hired one of racing's greats at the time, Lee Petty, in his Oldsmobile. Petty recalls those tests:

"Yeah, we went down there to West Palm and run two or three days, but we didn't find out much, I didn't think, but we didn't know a thing when we went there, so who knows. I knew they didn't have the right tires for the track we was runnin' at the time, and they knew it too. But they worked on it and—you know—they finally came up with a pretty good tire.

"There hadn't been much testin' of race tires at that time, unless you count runnin' 'em on the back roads at night and we sure done plenty of that. But they picked me because we had won most of the races. The fact that we stayed down there for as long as we did must have meant they were learnin' something.

"One thing is, we started when nobody knew a thing about it, so anything we found out was a big break. I run Goodyears most of the time after that; I mean, they didn't know a whole lot about building a race tire back then, but they sure knew a lot more than anybody else.

"They paid us some for the tests, but not a whole lot; it didn't matter because every little bit of money we got back in those days was a whole lot to us. Drivers actually signed with Goodyear or Firestone back then and you'd have to be loyal to the company who was payin' you."

One such driver was Buck Baker. He took the Goodyears that were available and won six races that year, which propelled him right into the national championship, garnering 10,716 points, which was the greatest number of points any NASCAR driver ever had gotten.

The following year, Lee Petty roared past that mark with 12,232 points to win his second of three Grand National (now Winston Cup) championships.

Other names were starting to emerge from the ranks; names that would become synonymous with speed and daring in stock automobiles—Fireball Roberts, Junior Johnson, Marvin Panch and a host of others. They had joined the ranks of the original heroes—Petty, Baker, Tim and Fonty Flock, Frank Mundy, Red Byron, Herb Thomas, Speedy Thompson and Curtis Turner.

The sport, as well as the tires, was in a "development" stage, there was no question. There was little or no planning, or even order, for that matter, in the pits. The timing was a hit-and-miss thing at best and the drivers fought off the track about as much as they did on it.

The scoring, needless to say, was anything but scientific. Originally one person was assigned to each car. He was given a cigar box with exactly the number of marbles in it as there were laps in the race. As his car crossed the start/finish line, he was supposed to take out a marble and toss it in a bucket in front of him. But some of the guys found out that if they distracted the guy next to them by saying something like "Look at that car over there," he could throw the marble in the other guy's cigar box.

By the end of the race, nobody was real sure *who* had won. That's what started a lot of the fights.

Buck Baker won the 1957 Grand National (now Winston Cup) Championship on Goodyears.

A bevy of modified race cars approach the North Turn in 1958 beach racing action at Daytona. The cars already through the turn are racing down U.S. Highway 1, the only paved portion of the course.

In one race, Lee Petty came into the pits to get the mud cleaned off his windshield because he couldn't even see the race track. His crew, which consisted of his twelve-year-old son, Richard, jumped on the hood with a wet rag and wiped away. Lee was looking out the driver's window to see when he could merge back into traffic when he took off. There was one slight problem: Richard had not finished his job.

He clung desperately to the windshield wipers as the car roared back into the fray. When Lee looked back to the track all he saw were two huge eyes staring him in the face. He roared around the track and back into the pits, where Richard slid to safety. The youngster was promptly ejected from the pits because a kid of that age wasn't supposed to be there in the first place. A few laps later he was back in the pits in time to see his daddy take the checkered flag.

It was in the midst of all of this confusion that Goodyear and Firestone were trying to outdo one another with race tires. One week it might be an all Goodyear show and then Firestone would come up with something new and the next week was theirs.

Never had there been such a war in racing as the Goodyear-Firestone battles.

In one of the old beach races at Daytona, Gober Sosebee, an Atlanta driver, thought he had won the 160-lap race, but Bill France and the NASCAR scorers had determined that he was a lap down. They awarded him eighth place. Sosebee, who was nicknamed the "Wild Indian," went into orbit.

Atlantan Gober Sosebee was one of the top early beach racers.

The argument that followed between Sosebee and France lasted for an hour. Finally, seeing that France was not going to back down, Sosebee looked him in the eye and said:

"I never knew your mother, Bill; I'm sure she was a fine lady, but what you are is an *acquired* son-of-a-bitch."

Goodyear had come enthusiastically into this mayhem and they, as well as France, fully intended to make something out of this sport. They could see the great future it had.

The incident was indicative of the period; racing was still pretty much of a dog-eat-dog affair.

A Major Victory

The 1959 Southern 500 at Darlington was perhaps the crescendo of Goodyear's early stock car program. The company had gone there loaded for bear. They had tested at the track earlier in the year, using several of the top NASCAR drivers.

Goodyear engineers were not only dedicated, but determined. The race began with the usual war-like tactics. There were cars going in all directions when the green flag dropped—up high, down low, bumping into each other. But the real battle had begun a few months before. Firestone, sensing that Goodyear "was here to stay," had doubled their engineering efforts on producing a tire that would send these upstarts back to their offices on East Market Street, Akron.

Goodyear was not going to give up easily. They tried every idea they knew—although engineering ideas were somewhat limited at the end of the Fifties.

On race day, the field was about even between Goodyear and Firestone, so it was too close to call among the media. But there was no question; Goodyear's presence was felt. After several lead changes, a lot of crashes, and some tire failure on both sides, Jim Reed put his Chevrolet out in front of the pack and zinged across the finish line at an average speed of 111.836 miles per hour, which was more than nine miles per hour faster than the record speed set by Fireball Roberts one year earlier.

Fireball Roberts accepts the winner's trophy at the 1959 Rebel 300 at Darlington.

What was the difference? Well, a lot of people said that it was the Goodyear tires Reed was riding on. Whatever the reason, it was the greatest stock car victory Goodyear had ever had and they didn't hide the light under a basket.

With "the big one" under their belts, Goodyear engineers were spurred on to even greater heights.

The race car that got Goodyear going. Jim Reed's Chevrolet won the 1959 Southern 500 at Darlington. It was Goodyear's first major stock car victory and spurred the company on to greater heights. Reed's speed was more than nine miles per hour faster than that of the previous year's winner.

Racing Involvement Expands

The stock car success at Darlington was so inspiring that it caused Goodyear to look in other directions. Now that they had taken on America's best racing tire company, maybe it was time to take a pot-shot at some of the great *world* powers. Sports car racing was the venue.

The international marques ran on standard-looking tires, but they were nationalistic: The British cars ran Dunlops, the Germans used Continentals and the Italians racers ran Pirellis. The Akron engineers took note that European racing tires appeared to be much like street tires, but with less tread depth and more carcass plies (layers of fabric). Although they didn't admit it, they obviously had dissected a few of the competition's products.

Road races were run wet or dry so tread pattern, they assumed, was vital to the racing tires of the day.

Through the Fifties there seemed to be little change in tires other than a move to nylon fabric. In general, racing tread patterns continued to be similar to those of street tires.

When Goodyear introduced its line of sports car tires in late 1959, the international racers were noticeably skeptical. Aside from a fiercely provincial attitude, they could only assume that the new tires were little, if any, better than those Firestone had produced for a few years. The Firestones were considered to be inferior by the sporty car crowd. Even among American drivers, there was a feeling that "foreign was better." After all, they were driving, for the most part, foreign cars, so they were caught up in the across-the-pond syndrome.

A Goodyear racing cord from 1920 compared to the new 1959 Sports Car Special.

Whether it was fact or snobbery is unclear.

Most Sports Car Club of America (SCCA) racing was done on street tires with only the fastest cars using pure racing tires. Michelin X radials were popular with club racers because they gave long wear and worked well in the rain, too. Radials at that time were somewhat of an oddity and presented a few problems. For one thing, they had an unpredictable breakaway reputation that could be reduced with higher air pressure, so there was always a lot of "experimenting" among the teams to get the most effective pressure.

European tires could be considered significantly ahead technically of any similar American tires if, for no other reason, than the fact that there were few speed limits in Europe outside city perimeters and road racing was the predominate form of automobile competition. These two factors prompted European tire manufacturers in the Fifties to produce what was considered to be a better tire.

American racing, which had begun on dirt horse tracks, tended to stick to oval tracks. There definitely were speed limits on the highways, so there had been little reason for a high-speed tire. Until Goodyear and Firestone locked horns.

The bottom line was that American tire companies concentrated on tread mileage, while European companies emphasized performance and wet weather characteristics. It is an accolade to Goodyear engineers that their new *Sports Car Special* tire worked as well as it did. American sports car efforts, thanks to Briggs Cunningham's cars and the Corvettes produced by Chevrolet, also helped Goodyear. They, of course, were as anxious as the Europeans to use tires made "at home." It was an all-American effort.

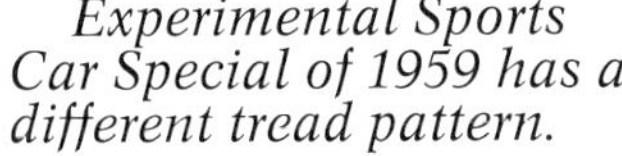

Experimental Sports Car Special of 1959 has a different tread pattern.

All these various directions of tire development, which had come to a head by the end of the Fifties, seemed to have little effect on the tire-buying public. The foreign car invasion, for example, led by sports cars after World War II, introduced the technologically-superior foreign street and high speed tires to the American market, but interest in these tires was limited exclusively to the people who owned the sports cars.

With speed limits in effect, it did not seem that American tire, manufacturers were paying attention. This was not true at Goodyear; the company was determined to make an impression on those who wanted a high performance tire. It wasn't really necessary at that point because their major market, the American automobile manufacturer, was not demanding a product other than it be round and able to hold their cars up in the showroom.

It didn't matter; there was a core of resolute engineers who knew that the high performance tire would someday make a difference, not only in tire sales but in company image. They felt strongly that

Goodyear's appearance was far too conservative. It needed a good shot in the arm.

Aside from the sports car crowd which knew about European performance tires, probably the most significant push for performance American tires came from California hot-rodders. Drag racing pioneered wide rims, oversized tires and slick retreads with traction compounds. High speed runs on the dry lake beds of Southern California and at the Bonneville Salt Flats created new challenges for which Firestone had already begun building special tires. But there were a few pioneer hot-rodders on the West Coast who knew what Goodyear was doing with stock and sports cars and they camped on Goodyear's doorstep, asking for an even better tire than the ones being supplied by Firestone.

One of the first was Dean Moon, who had trailblazed a dozen hot-rodding concepts in California. He called Goodyear and asked if some of their engineers could come out to Muroc Dry Lake to "just watch what we're doing with cars."

There was no doubt that California had taken the world lead in outright straightaway speed. In fact, a whole new world of speed had been created, one that was to become a mainstay of the racing industry.

Suddenly Goodyear was up to its corporate ears in far more forms of auto racing than they had ever imagined possible.

It looked as if the conservative image of the company was beginning to change. A sort of chrysalis was emerging.

More than Tread Patterns?

Although it wasn't a sports car that caused engineers to look toward compounding as an integral part of racing tire development, it was a sports car track that led to it. In 1959, the United States Auto Club (USAC) had scheduled a midget race at Watkins Glen, New York on the road course. Midgets on a road course was odd enough, but to add to that, it rained and they elected to go ahead and run, although midgets never ran in the rain on their customary oval tracks.

"It'll be a great show," proclaimed USAC. Most American racing was done on dry tracks, thus rubber compounding was for heat and wear only, with traction of somewhat less importance. This was also the case for passenger car tires at the time with most testing going on at Goodyear's test track at San Angelo, Texas, and Firestone's track at Fort Stockton, Texas.

The race at Watkins Glen lived up to USAC's billing: Most of those guys had never even turned *right* much less driven in the rain. They ran the race on slick tires and, primarily because of their skill, matched the times of the sports cars which ran on tires with patterned treads.

Not many who weren't there paid much attention to the feat the drivers had accomplished, but it suggested, to Firestone at least, that compound might play a role in traction and not tread pattern as all tire companies believed. After all, they reasoned, it is the rubber on the pavement that sticks you to the track, not the air in the grooves.

Later in 1959, Rodger Ward, who had won the Indianapolis 500 that year, proved that a softer compound helped stick the car to the track. The race was held at the road course in Lime Rock, Connecticut, and Ward was there with his midget, to challenge the best sports cars in the world. After swapping the lead several times with Chuck Daigh in the Camoradi Formula I Maserati 250F and George Constantine in an Aston Martin DBR1, Ward surged to the front in his midget with Firestone slicks and nobody ever caught him.

There was less attention being paid to sports car racing in those days, so the incident all but went unnoticed. The compounding issue was put on the back burner for a while.

Fast Tracks Challenge Engineers

The era of the superspeedway began in earnest in 1959 when Bill France realized his dream of building the most modern racing facility in the world. But before the Daytona International Speedway opened its gates to the public, both Goodyear and Firestone realized that they would have to do some serious tire testing, primarily because this new track was sure to be the fastest in the world.

The Daytona tri-oval track was two and one-half miles around—the same as Indianapolis—but the towering thirty-one-degree banks meant that cars could go through the turns nearly as fast as they could go down the straightaway. It was wide and fast, and this increased the possibility of tire problems.

The tests were somewhat less than conclusive. The drivers all wanted the experience of running on the new track so there was no lack of interest on their part; it was just that France was behind schedule and they were working on the track almost until the time of the first qualifying races.

"We would get out there and run a few laps, sometimes around construction equipment, and then they'd shut us down so they could work more on the track," recalls Walt DeVinney. "They actually built a track around us. We didn't learn too much because we'd get in a few laps and then they would stop us to put up some more guard rail or something. Neither Goodyear nor Firestone really had any testing that meant anything because we couldn't put together enough consecutive laps to prove a thing."

Walt DeVinney, one of the early Goodyear racing geniuses, pictured in 1959.

As it turned out, both companies's tires proved satisfactory for the tremendous speeds. Fans poured into the grand new facility from all over the Southeast. The sandy parking lots steadily filled as the people arrived for Speed Week 1959. But before most of them arrived, tragedy struck the new speedway. One of the early beach and NASCAR stars, Marshall Teague, was driving Chapman Root's modified Indianapolis car, the *Sumar Special*, in practice runs around the new track. The streamlined car had looked good the first couple of times around the tri-oval, but suddenly as it went into the second turn at 160 miles per hour, it lurched into a broadslide and began to flip. It spewed parts all over the course as it spun dizzily five times in mid air, landing 500 yards from the point where it had started to flip. The seat, with Teague still in it, tore loose while the car was still flipping and landed 150 feet ahead of the chassis. Teague was found harnessed to the seat. Daytona's great local hero had been killed instantly.

As the late model stock cars arrived, they seemed to form a sort of memorial to Teague, who had been with them from the beginning. And these cars were just the sensation the fans had expected on the high banks. It was obvious that Bill France had once more made the right decision in building the Daytona International Speedway.

Along with the seasoned veterans of beach and dirt track racing and Darlington—the original superspeedway for stock cars—came a young man who was to make the most profound impression on stock car racing of anybody in history. His name was Richard Lee Petty.

Richard had raced one season in the convertible class, but this was to be his inaugural year in the Grand National (Winston Cup) circuit. It would, in effect, pit Petty against Petty. Richard against Lee.

It didn't take long for the cars to roar past the beach course records. Cotton Owens in a 1958 Pontiac turned the fastest Daytona 500 qualifying time of 143.198, which was astounding considering that this was his average all the way around the two and one-half mile track. The record for the beach had been set by Paul Goldsmith the year before, also in a 1958 Pontiac. He had been clocked at 140.570, but that had been in a straightaway run with no turns.

Shorty Rollins in a Ford won the first stock car race at the new track, a one hundred mile qualifying event. Bob Welborn in a Chevrolet won the second one-hundred-miler.

The stage was set for the first Daytona 500.

If Bill France had been able to write a script for the race, it could not have been more exciting: Fifty-nine gleaming cars roared away as the starter dropped the green flag. Welborn, Tom Pistone and Little Joe Weatherly battled back and forth for the lead for the first twenty-two laps. Fireball Roberts took over for the next twenty laps and from then on, it was a series of lead changes and excitement that kept the crowd on its feet for most of the race.

Firestone tires had been slightly faster in qualifying, so many of the top drivers were running them. But the Goodyears were holding their own. There were quite a few tire problems but neither Firestone nor Goodyear had a performance edge in the initial Daytona 500.

Lee Petty in his Olds 88 took the lead at the 375-mile mark and five laps later Johnny Beauchamp eased past in his Ford Thunderbird. After that, it was a seesaw battle for the rest of the race, with Petty leading one lap and Beauchamp the next. On the last lap, Petty, Beauchamp and Weatherly (who was one lap down) roared down the tri-oval in front of the grandstands three abreast. They ran wheel-to-wheel through the high banks of the west turns and down the back straightaway. The three cars roared through turns three and four as if they were welded together, not one of them giving an inch.

They thundered across the finish line in what appeared to be a dead heat. Of course, the winner would be either Petty or Beauchamp because of Weatherly's one lap down situation. Still he kept charging.

At first Beauchamp was thought to be the winner. And then Petty.

Cotton Owens, left, receives trophy after winning 1953 100-miler at Daytona. Second place finisher Ralph Moody, center, looks on as Diane Davis of Chicago makes presentation.(top photo)

Three of racing's early greats are shown in the photo above: Ralph Moody, half of famed Holman-Moody racing team, left; Bob Colvin, president of Darlington Raceway, center, and Little Joe Weatherly.

Lee Petty, left, displays the checkered flag and the typical driving attire of the period.

But there was no use, they would have to rely on the photograph of the finish—and even then it took *three days* of studying it before the NASCAR panel finally declared Lee Petty the winner of the first Daytona 500. Richard had finished a disappointing 57th because of mechanical problems, but his career in Grand National racing was underway. And it was to become an achievement that nobody will ever forget, nor probably ever match.

Richard's impressions of the new speedway seemed to echo those of the other drivers, but, being a rookie, his were perhaps a little more objective. He has this to say:

"I had just as much chance in that race as anyone; in fact, being a rookie might have given me a slight edge. The deal was, *nobody* knew anything about driving that big oval, so we were starting even—just like Daddy had in the first Grand National race at Charlotte ten years before. But my *edge* was due to the fact that I didn't have to *unlearn* as many short track habits. The track gave some of the old-timers a fit, but it was all new to me, so, for once, not knowing anything was a blessing.

"If they decided to run on the inside of the track and I decided I could go better on the outside, my guess was as good as theirs. In fact, most drivers ran just like they did on other tracks, where the groove was on the inside; it wasn't there at Daytona."

Richard Petty also discovered another interesting phenomenon in the race, although it took him—and the other drivers, who must have experienced the same thing—a while to realize what the oddity was.

"I first noticed the effect when I was running off the banks to keep up with the pack," says Petty. "Every once in a while I would go whizzing right by them like they had stopped, and then, just a little later, they would come flying by me—the whole pack I had just blown off. I said 'Man, there's something going on here.' I didn't know what it was then, but I began experimenting and found a place where my car was running faster than anybody's—a spot where I could get by.

"I would follow the pack close through the corner. Then, when we came out of the turn, I would pull out and go right on by them. I was getting a sling-shot effect. I was actually catching a draft but didn't know it."

What Petty had discovered, of course, is what all cars do today on the longer tracks—drafting.

A young Richard Petty leads father Lee Petty in the 1960 Southern 500 at Darlington.

"I was a little puzzled with this deal," says Petty, "but I didn't say a word about it to anybody, not even Daddy. But I watched him from the pits after I had gone out, and I could see just as clear as day that they were doing the same thing. It was why one of them would lead one lap and the other the next. They were drafting. I thought, 'Man, this is some deal. It's gonna' win me some races.' "

Nobody ever disputed his logic.

Richard Petty gets ready to race at Darlington in 1960.

Camoradi, Brabham and the T-16 compound were Goodyear breakthroughs of the Sixties

Everything was rolling for Goodyear. Example: Lance Reventlow was developing his racing Scarab, with Goodyear involvement; they were cars that had previously been successful in the United States on Firestones.

Much early Goodyear sports car tire development took place with Scarabs at Riverside, California in the fall of 1959. To overcome wheelspin on acceleration, like the drag racers, the Scarab crew wanted a wider tire with no increase in diameter. Walt DeVinney inserted a spacer in the mold of a nominal 670-15, which widened the tire to almost eight inches. It was close to an aspect ratio of seventy, while most other tires were about eighty.

A.J. Foyt roars to victory in the 1963 Nassau Governor's Trophy Road Race in John Mecom's Scarab.

Testing of this revolutionary new low-profile tire on the Scarabs provided significantly faster lap times on the tight Riverside road course.

But perhaps the biggest breakthrough was when the Camoradi USA Racing Team was formed in 1959. The objective was simple: challenge the Europeans with the best sports cars they could buy and use the best drivers they could hire, leaning as heavily as possible to Americans, but not exclusively. They fully intended to dominate the 1960 International Championship for Makes sports car championship. Goodyear became the team's first sponsor.

Lucky Casner had put together the Camoradi team, dreaming up the immodest name (CAsner MOtor RAcing DIvision). At the Havana Grand Prix in 1960, the lead Camoradi entry was the new Type 61 Birdcage Maserati with Stirling Moss at the wheel. DeVinney took along four new experimental tires, each with a different tread design. Moss tested them all and selected a tread pattern that became a front-runner for years and is still available for vintage racers.

Stirling Moss pilots one of the Camoradi Birdcage Maseratis.

Camoradi gave Goodyear access to some of the top drivers in the world. It was a wonderful foot-in-the-door for them to jump into the international motorsports fray.

More importantly for the United States, it had provided enthusiasts with their biggest boost for international accomplishment since Briggs Cunningham stopped assaulting LeMans with his home-builts in the mid-Fifties. The Orsi family, who ran Maserati, thought highly enough of Camoradi to be willing to entrust it with the job of reviving Officine Maserati as a respected name on the road circuits. Goodyear also tied in much of its future as a developer of road racing tires with Camoradi's performance.

Camoradi's Birdcage Maseratis led both the Buenos Aires 1000 Kilometer (Argentina) and the 12 Hours of Sebring (Florida) championship endurance races until the too-delicate units broke. Casner planned to withdraw the *Tipo 61*'s from the Italian Targa Florio and the 1000-kilo at Nurburgring, Germany, but with help from the Maserati factory, he decided to enter both races, resulting in a near-win at Targa and a Stirling Moss/Dan Gurney clear-cut victory at Nurburgring.

The effort was not only a god-send for Goodyear but one for the Orsi family, as well. They had been beset with financial woes but were determined to get the familiar trident logo back into international competition. Oddly, it was an American effort that did just that.

It had all begun in Modena, Italy, in a luncheon at which the Chianti flowed. When Casner left, he had a charter to operate Camoradi as the official Maserati works team in International Championship for Makes events throughout the world.

This gave his group an advantage few private teams ever enjoy. They were guaranteed the latest factory-fresh cars and the backing of Maserati's technical group. In addition, they received front-line help from Maserati's chief mechanic Guarino Bertocchi, engineer Antonio Alfieri and team manager Nello Ugolini, whose pedigree included organizing stop-watch strategy for both Maserati and Ferrari.

Here's how the super team came together: shortly after an Aston Martin DBR-1 won the Tourist Trophy at Goodwood, England and with it the 1959 European Championship for Touring Cars, David Brown announced that the Astons would not be around in 1960. This decree left Moss and Carroll Shelby among the unemployed. Realizing that neither would remain without a ride for long, Casner set the diplomatic wheels in motion and by Nassau Speed Week in December, he had Shelby signed as a regular. Moss then agreed to a part-time driving schedule in selected events.

Prior to the inaugural United States Grand Prix at Sebring, Florida, two things happened to Dan Gurney: he broke his foot in a karting accident at Nassau and had a disagreement with the Ferrari hierarchy about his 1960 contract, so he started searching "help wanted" ads for people interested in young American chauffeurs.

Casner pinched himself when he heard Gurney was available and went into a huddle with him at Sebring in late December. They worked out an agreement that would not conflict with the young Californian's commitment to drive Formula I with the British BRM team the following season.

Another bonus came in the form of American Masten Gregory, who had been dropped by Jaguar. Camoradi also drew the attention of a New Zealand jewel, Bruce McLaren.

With such an array of talent, Goodyear decided to take on the world. They had locked horns with Firestone in the United States on the stock car circuit but had no strong sports car or European program. Camoradi gave them the opportunity. It was a fantasy come true: here was a team with outstanding cars and some of the best drivers in the world. And a Goodyear contract.

Briggs Cunningham, left, reminisces at Sebring 1971 with Gentleman Jim Kimberley, right, as unidentified young woman enjoys the yarns.

Bill Krause takes the checker at 1960 LA Times GP at Riverside after driving this Birdcage Maserati to victory.

This is the new Sports Car Special which carried the Maserati to victory.

Goodyear's general manager of racing, Tony Webner, immediately sent Goodyear technicians to the world sports car events, so the company's presence in Europe wouldn't go unnoticed.

There were as many as eight Camoradi cars in some events, and victories were not uncommon.

It was an opportunity that was all but handed to Goodyear, whose racing people stood in the wings, ready to pounce on any and all world competition, regardless of venue. Up to that point they weren't exactly sure *where* to jump. Or when.

Next, Casner went to Zora Arkus-Duntov, father of the Corvette, and lined up some of the Chevrolet sports cars.

Zora Arkus-Duntov, left, father of the Corvette, shown here in 1974 victory circle helping John Greenwood celebrate his IMSA *win at Daytona.*

"We are, after all, an all-American operation," Casner pointed out, "so we'll use American cars whenever possible. Unfortunately there's nothing made in this country that we can use in the three-liter sports/racing class, so we'll also stick with the Maseratis.

"We've been kidded about using Moss as a driver because he isn't American," Casner mused, "but what would you do if he were available? We feel," he dead-panned, "that it is better to have Stirling with us than against us."

It's the kind of reasoning that made the team a success and, in so doing, planted the Goodyear flag firmly on foreign racing soil, in mortal combat with Dunlop, Pirelli and Firestone.

Importance of Compounds

As the Tire War heated-up, Goodyear engineers began to look back to the 1959 Lime Rock race when Rodger Ward had beaten some of the fastest cars in the world in his midget. The engineers analyzed the situation and decided that compounding, after all, might make the difference they desired.

Ward had beaten the big European racers with slicks on his midget so they knew that tread design alone wasn't the answer.

Compounding in the early Sixties mainly used only natural rubber, in three hardnesses. For Goodyear it was: T-2 (the code designation of one of the early concoctions) for long wear; T-3, the all-around wear and traction choice and T-4, which was a very soft rubber for rain.

As Goodyear began to enter more and more European events, the need for rain tires became greater. It was wet during the 1960 running of the French classic—the 24 Hours of LeMans. The T-4s worked well; they went through the corners quickly and appeared to be competitive with the European tires. On the other hand, the three Cunningham Corvettes on Firestones were virtually undrivable in the rain. Two of them crashed and one survived to finish eighth overall.

Goodyear's Camoradi Corvette ran the entire race on one set of tires and finished tenth, which was outstanding for a showroom stock car. Camoradi's Maseratis led the race, set the fastest lap and fastest three-liter straightaway speed of 169 miles per hour but failed to finish because of mechanical and electrical woes.

Leo Mehl, who was hired in 1962 as a tire engineer, and Ron Gries spent most of the fall of 1963 doing theoretical exercises in racing design. The pot was boiling in Akron.

"We did all kinds of basic stuff," says Mehl. "We put straight circumferential grooves around and around; we put them at different widths and different depths; then we put them at forty-five-degree and ninety-degree angles across the tire.

"Our people also were working on constructions. With the bias-ply tire, the more air you put in them, the rounder they got, so, in an effort to get more tread on the ground and thereby get more grip, they designed a flat tread. When you did that, of course, you got a tremendous amount of rubber piled-up in the shoulder, and this was one of the places that the temperature really happened; shoulders would chunk off, particularly the inside, so we had some pretty hairy days at the track.

"I heard some wild stories from guys like Jim Loulan, who was in charge of race tire development. They actually took the tires out on the backroads on Saturday nights, running them on rental cars, trying to wear them down because they knew that come Sunday they would blister and chunk if they didn't get some of the rubber worn away, allowing the tire to dissipate the heat better the next day. They were primitive —and exciting—times." Certainly unorthodox.

Carroll Shelby's fierce Cobras are prepared for battle in the 1963 Nassau Trophy Race.

It was time to return, once more, to the drawing board. "At the lab we were doing all these basic designs, probably thirty, and we went to Daytona to test them," says Mehl. "We had them built with one compound, so we could tell how well each particular design worked. Carroll Shelby brought his Cobras to Florida following the Nassau Road Races in December. Ken Miles was our driver.

"We got a water truck and wet down the infield course at Daytona," Mehl continues. "The results were pretty upsetting. We had spent three months doing this whole test and all of the tires seemed to be the same. We weren't making any progress at all; not a single set of tires was faster than the one before. All Ron Gries's and Elmer Wasko's designs were about the same.

Drivers streak for the cars and the LeMans start at the 1963 Nassau Governor's Trophy Road Race in the Bahamas. Most of the cars, including the mighty Cobras and the factory Corvettes, ran on Goodyear Sports Car Specials.

Dan Gurney (Car 69) in 1963 VW race at Nassau. Car owners Roger Penske, left, and John Mecom cheer Gurney on to victory by such a wide margin that the car was impounded and disqualified for having a Porsche engine—a comic gesture by Mecom and Penske who knew they would be found out.

"Bill Robinson was our racing tire distributor in Florida and he kept needling me about a tire he had 'built.' He said, 'I've got a tire that will blow all you big time engineers in the weeds.' I ignored him as long as I could because all he had done was take a regular passenger car tire and had a service station man in Fort Lauderdale recap it. It had no sloping grooves, no place for the water to flow. I said, 'You don't want to put those things on, you'll kill the guy out there in the rain.' He said 'You just try it and see.'

"So just to shut him up, we put them on. They were about three seconds faster than anything we had. We had spent three days and couldn't get one second out of our tires and here Bill had added three seconds, just like that.

"This retread with all the grooves closed *was* blowing us in the weeds. We couldn't understand, and then it finally dawned on us that it didn't make any difference what kind of grooves we had if the compound didn't have any grip."

The light came on.

"We went back and started figuring what compound didn't have any bite, so we started taking stuff out and putting other stuff in, and this is how we really started to become competitive," Mehl recalls.

What also stimulated this wet performance interest was a result of Dan Gurney taking a set of stock car tires to England to race on a Ford

Galaxie he and Jack Brabham were running in the British Tourist Trophy championship event. "I told Dan not to run them in the rain," says Fred Gamble, who by then was running Goodyear's European racing operation, "but in a race at Brands Hatch, Brabham got caught in a downpour and spun the car into the shrubbery. To say the least, the press coverage of this American tire threat was extremely caustic and an embarrassment to Goodyear Great Britain. They complained loudly to management in Akron—'You bloody Yanks are not helping us much.' "

Goodyear went back to Daytona to test, with some new compounds. This time the driver was Davey MacDonald. In a Cobra. The sequence was to dive into the braking area, corner and accelerate out for a timed segment of about twelve seconds per test.

"All of the test tires performed similarly, visually sliding on braking, wheel-spinning through the corner and having trouble with traction accelerating out," recalls Gamble. "The straight-grooved tires were a couple tenths [of a second] quicker than the other patterns. This proved to us that straight circumferential grooves were the significant tread design element for wet traction."

Carroll Shelby, left, gives last minute instructions to Ken Miles at Sebring, 1964.

Everybody was prepared to do any job in the early days. Here Leo Mehl checks the right front tire.

It was back to the laboratory to work more on compounds.

To make a compound, large quantities of rubber and carbon black and oils and bonders are put in a huge Banbury mixer. It's a lot like mixing the batter for a very large cake—a 500 pound one. But the racing tire compounders had a tiny Banbury in the lab and they could mix batches as small as three pounds.

They mixed up many different compounds and made a lot of blocks and strips of the rubber. They then performed all sorts of tests that would tell them how hard it was, how much grip it got, how much tensile strength it had, how much it was likely to tear and how it would process in the factory.

With the small Banbury, Mehl and the other compounders could predict all of the properties of a particular mixture. They put in a little more of this and took out some of that until BINGO! they came up with a compound they dubbed "T-16."

"The T-16 was the phenomenal compound for NASCAR," says Mehl.

Goodyear-clad Cobra Daytona coupe races on towards night at the 1964 12 Hours of Sebring.

The Goodyear blimp Mayflower *passes over the Firestone tire area at Sebring, 1965.*

"It was the breakthrough of the century in racing. It was heat-resistant, wore extremely well, and it was tear-resistant and didn't chunk or blister like some of the others. We intended it for short track use, but you know racers—they never do anything they're told to do. First they used them at Darlington and then on sports cars, and I'll be damned if it didn't work everyplace. On any car.

"It was so good that every compounder claimed to have developed it, so we're still not real sure who did it. It may have been a joint effort."

For the first time, all tire companies realized that compounding was important. Prior to that, designers had been changing the widths and heights and designs and had never given much thought to compounds.

Goodyear's T-16 compound changed that for all time.

Phil Hill, left, America's first Formula I champion, and Pedro Rodriguez display the winner's trophy after the 1964 Daytona Continental, forerunner of today's Rolex 24.

Bill France, Jr., left, with Dan Gurney at Daytona in 1965.(below)

Tires for LeMans

Sports car racing has long provided one of the most prestigious and well-supported fields of play in motorsports. One of the oldest single events, the 24 Hours of LeMans, was first held in 1923, but, over the years, there have been many challenging sports car races added to the world racing calendar, including the 12 Hours of Sebring and 24 Hours of Daytona.

The very essence of sports car racing has always been centered upon endurance. Durability. The early years were dominated by Ferrari and other specialist sports/racing car manufacturers. Later, with the advent of commercialism, several other marques began to realize the benefits and started playing an active role in the burgeoning sports car championship.

Nevertheless, the mid-Fifties to mid-Sixties continue to be regarded by many as the zenith for sports car racing. The battles among Aston Martin, Cunningham, Ferrari, Jaguar, Maserati, Mercedes-Benz and Porsche yielded intense competition with exciting and largely unrestricted machinery. Even so, most could be—and often were—driven on the road.

International sports car racing has always been a consummate arena in which to highlight the performance of a high performance tire. Goodyear engineers realized this from the beginning, because the race was not only designed to test the limits of car and driver but the endurance of equipment as well.

Jaguars and Aston Martins had ruled the sports car roost for awhile and then they departed, leaving the whole affair to Ferrari and Porsche for several years. Along the way, when the Americans got in the scene with Camoradi, it had become a different story, resulting in the 1960 Nurburgring victory of Moss and Gurney piloting their Birdcage Maserati to victory, and bringing Goodyear its first world championship sports car win.

But by 1963, prototype car engine regulations were revised, controlled not by size but by a sliding scale of minimum weights—similar to that currently in use in the International Motor Sports Association's Camel GT Championship.

This change had the desirable effect of attracting the Ford Motor Company, Carroll Shelby, Goodyear and General Motors. International racing was rapidly becoming a hotbed of activity in the United States.

The prototype cars were enveloped formally within the International Championship for Makes in 1964, and two years later the mighty seven-liter Ford GT MkIIs swept to victory at LeMans. On Goodyears. But it wasn't an easy accomplishment for Goodyear.

John Wyer was in charge Ford's LeMans operation, having previously led Aston Martin to a string of victories. John Hartz was Goodyear's director of development and he, as well as board chairman DeYoung, was sick of the Firestone victories. DeYoung gave Hartz the order, "Beat those guys." Hartz took it seriously, as well he should, so he turned to Leo Mehl and said, "Everybody is going to be looking to Indianapolis and Daytona and all the other races, so you're in charge of developing a compound for LeMans."

John Wyer, team manager for the Ford factory effort at LeMans in the Sixties.

It was a big order, but Mehl proved that he was up to it. Hartz added, "Leo, we want to win this one, so do whatever you have to do. If anybody gives you any static, you come straight to me."

It was the first *carte blanche* "spend all that it takes" order that had been issued. Ford and Goodyear were committed to winning LeMans, though each for their own reasons.

"We followed Shelby through the 1964 season, changing designs and compounds and making notes. And we won the 12 Hours of Sebring," says Mehl, "so in April we went to LeMans to test. Everything seemed great."

Ford and Shelby took twelve cars to LeMans. "I guess I was a little naive," says Mehl. "We had the best tires, so what was there to worry about?"

But it wasn't tires that caused the problem. Goodyear had been using stick-on wheel weights and had found that it didn't matter how fast a car went, they stayed in place, mostly by centrifugal force. Prior to that, they had found that clip-on weights often flew off at speeds over 150 miles per hour.

"When we got there," Mehl recalls, "the service guys from Wolverhampton said they had a new wheel weight that was fantastic. No problems at all. I was skeptical at first because I knew the Ford GTs would be hitting about 240 miles an hour on the Mulsanne Straight, where there was a slight kink in the course. It was extremely dangerous. There were no guard rails, just a row of big, solid sycamore trees—a sort of tunnel of trees you had to run through. There had been a lot of drivers killed there over the years.

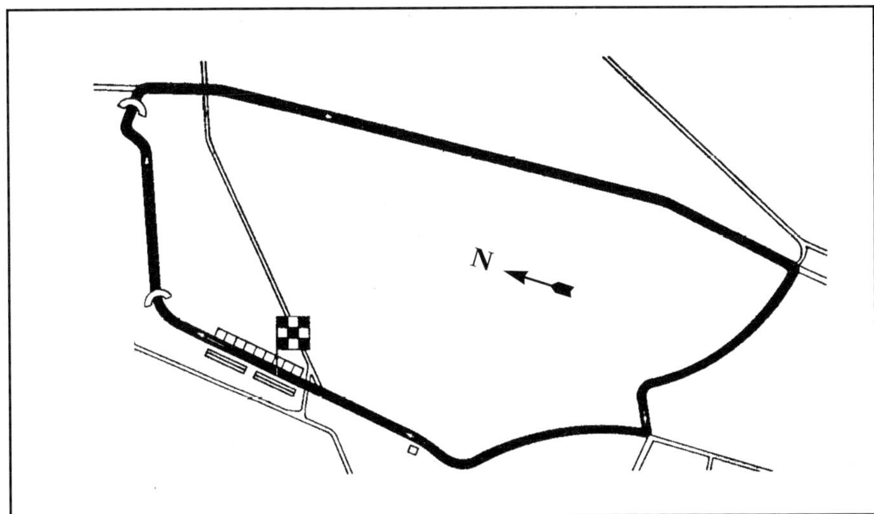

The LeMans Circuit, 8.38 miles in length, 1964.

"But they finally convinced me to use the weights," Mehl says with a chagrined look on his face.

On the first day of practice, there were six Cobras with fiberglass bodies and six GTs with aluminum skins. There were twenty-four of the finest drivers in the world, including Dan Gurney, Phil Hill, Bruce McLaren and Bob Bondurant.

"They went charging out at the start of the initial practice session in a great roar and, after the first eight-mile lap, in came three drivers, madder than hell," says Mehl. "Two Cobras had these big bumps in the

The first win for the Cobra Daytona coupe, LeMans 1964, with Bob Bondurant and Dan Gurney at the wheel. They finished 1st in GT Class, 4th overall.

front fenders and one GT40 had a big hole in the right front fender. The wheel weights had come off in the Mulsanne Straight and scared the hell out of the drivers. A weight was stuck into the firewall two inches from one driver's head—and it happened at 200 mph. The next lap six more came in. Everybody was screaming 'Goodyear. Goodyear.' And I was there all alone.

"Phil Remington was Shelby's chief engineer, so he and I grabbed pliers and started pulling off the remaining weights. Race tires are fairly well balanced anyway, so we figured we were better off with none than running the risk of crashing a car."

They got the cars through practice and then went back to the stick-on wheel weights.

When Goodyear went to LeMans for the 1965 race, all of the Cobras had 289 engines, very fast and very reliable. But Shelby also had some back-up engines that had been bored out to 325. They weren't as reliable, but they were faster. And, if that wasn't enough, he had two 427 Holman-Moody stock car engines. Obviously they had the power but there was serious doubt that they could last twenty-four hours. It didn't matter, Ford's orders had been "get the pole." Shelby intended to do just that, no matter what it took.

The Ferraris proved faster in practice, so Shelby put in the 325s. They were faster but the suspension wasn't right for them, so his chassis and suspension man, Carroll Smith, stayed up all night getting the cars set up right.

The next day they still weren't as fast as the Ferraris. "Put in the 427s," Shelby commanded. "Are you sure?" questioned Smith. "Put 'em in," Shel said.

That's when Mehl realized they had a serious tire problem. With the big engines, the cars had a lot of negative camber, like an old VW with the top of the tires in and the bottom out. The inside shoulder was going to take a tremendous beating.

"I was concerned because I knew they had increased the tread depth from 8/32 of an inch to 12/32. It meant heat build-up. But the only visible difference was the new tread design. Instead of being the traditional 'diamond,' it was one that looked like an 'S.'

"In practice, the end of the 'S' was extending. It was tearing. Pretty soon the 'S' would connect with another 'S.' When they dumped in the 427s, the problem was greatly increased because the suspension had sort of collapsed and the inside shoulder of the tire was taking a tremendous beating.

"I was just an engineer," Mehl says, "so I did what Shelby and the Ford guys told me to do. But I did plan to change tires more often than everybody thought necessary, just to be sure."

Phil Hill sat on the pole with one of the 427s, which made the American contingent very happy. But, following qualifying, Mehl put some of the tires in his car trunk and took Shelby out into the far reaches of the infield where nobody could see them. He told Shelby, "We have a serious problem, Shel." And he showed him the tearing tread. "What's the answer?" Shelby asked.

"There isn't any real answer," Mehl said. "The only thing we can do is run on used tires, ones that have some of the rubber already worn off. It will dissipate the heat more. Besides," Mehl added, "this track is so slick that the tires won't wear out anyway. I assure you."

"All right, run the used ones," Shelby said. At the start of the race, Hill took a commanding lead. Every hour they came in for gas. Mehl carefully checked the tires. Hour one, they were fine. Hour two, the same. After the third hour, Mehl went to the stands where Shelby and Henry Ford II were sitting and said, "It looks like the tires are going to work, so we're not planning a change until about two in the morning." "Fine," said Shelby.

When Mehl got back to the pits Hill had just come in. Mehl jumped over the wall and checked the tires again. He casually looked at the left rear. Something didn't look right. He looked again, and, in the dim light, he saw what had happened. He was looking at a tire *carcass*. There was no tread at all. It had come off completely and looked just like a slick.

A 1965 Sports Car Special.

"I realized that if he went back out there and made it to the Mulsanne Straight and got up to 240 [mph], he wasn't coming back. They already had been in the pits for four minutes and they wanted badly to retain their lead, but I ran to Shelby and pulled him by the arm. 'You've gotta' change the left rear,' I screamed to him.

"They changed it, but in the process, they lost the lead. Then all hell broke loose. Every Ford came in with treads missing. We kept changing tires and the cars remained in contention but I knew we were sitting on a time bomb."

Fortunately for Goodyear and unfortunately for Ford, all of their cars went out; the 427s with gear box failures because there was just too much power, and the others with head gasket problems. It saved Goodyear, in a way.

Few ever knew how close Goodyear and Ford had come to disaster on the track. But the story had a happy ending for Goodyear. Luigi Chinetti had spoken with John Hartz, who had promised him tires for LeMans for his 275LM Ferrari. When he came to Mehl in the pits before practice, Mehl knew nothing about the promise. In fact, he didn't even have any tires that would work on the Ferrari. Chinetti had already had a disagreement with Dunlop and they wouldn't give him any tires, so Mehl began to ponder the problem. With all of the tearing problems, the last thing Mehl needed was somebody else screaming at him.

He remembered a skinny rain tire that he had brought for the Cobras. It would fit, so he offered it to Chinetti. The tire had been used successfully by Brabham and Jimmy Clark in various rain situations, but not on the dry. It was all Goodyear had to offer.

Mehl told Chinetti that he could use "these tires," and he accepted. "But you'd better have a strong pit crew because you'll have to change them every hour," he warned Chinetti. Mehl forgot all about the 275, what with all of the Ford problems, but when he awoke from a nap at four in the morning the car was running third.

Masten Gregory co-drove Chinetti's Ferrari in 1965, bringing Goodyear its first overall victory at LeMans.

"I thought 'this is pretty amazing; we might get third after all.' " recalls Mehl. "They had two drivers—Masten Gregory and Jochen Rindt; Masten was known as 'Crashin' Masten' and Rindt as 'the Wild Man.' They were the last two drivers anybody thought could finish an endurance race."

As it turned out, the pair drove flawlessly. And frantically. But the car was in the pits for nearly an hour, so Rindt went to his passenger car to leave the track. The car was blocked in, so while he was waiting for a wrecker to move some cars, one of his crew members came running over and said, "Get back over there. The car's fixed and they need you."

In typical racer fashion, Rindt got in the car and said "Well, if this thing's going to break again, let's break it now." He drove like a mad man and, because the tires didn't have much grip, the car held together.

With about one hour to go, they had gotten up to second place. Mehl was dazed.

"When the lead car hit the curb about six miles from the finish, my

A rare photo of the winning Cobra Daytona team at LeMans in 1964. The car finished first in GT class, fourth overall. From left: Carroll Shelby, Dan Gurney, Bob Bondurant and actor Peter Ustinov.

jaw dropped to the ground," Mehl says. "We had won the race. The 24 Hours of LeMans!"

They changed twenty-four sets of the rain tires and when the checkered flag dropped, the 275 had won. As had Goodyear.

"I'll never forget my telephone conversation with John Hartz after the race," he recalls. "I was sitting in my motel room. I hadn't really slept in three days and was near an ulcer from the strain, but we had won.

"John [Hartz] was an ever-positive guy, so I said, 'John, you just can't believe what happened over here.' 'What?' he asked, half in wonderment and half in fear. I said, 'Well, we chunked tires, we threw treads, we blistered, we tore up about everything, all the Fords blew up, but something really strange happened.' He said, this time with great concern: 'What?'

"We won the race," Mehl told him, "In Luigi's car." And then he asked: "Do you remember telling him I would supply him with tires?"

Hartz said, 'Yeah, I remember that.'

Mehl asked, "Do you...remember ever telling me that?"

There was a pause. John meekly replied: "Well, no I don't."

End of conversation.

What European racing had in style, NASCAR made up for in true grit.

It was not over for Ford. Nor Goodyear. They both would roar back in the next two years to completely dominate LeMans and to temporarily demoralize Enzo Ferrari, which had been Henry Ford II's prime goal in the first place—ever since Ferrari had refused to sell out to Ford. If Ford couldn't own Ferrari, he would beat them on the race track where Ferrari had reigned supreme for years.

With the sweet smell of success in its nostrils, Goodyear decided to get the company more firmly entrenched into international racing. Building of racing tires for Europe had been moved to Goodyear's British operation at Wolverhampton, because the company was so intent on making its mark in Europe that it felt the need to be "closer to the continental action."

Due to the all-weather racing in Europe, Goodyear's *forte* again became rubber compounding. The initial emphasis had been placed upon Shelby's Cobra effort, so it was through the Texas racer/entrepreneur that Goodyear became involved in the Ford LeMans campaign, which was one of the most successful efforts in motorsports history.

Ford, which had been so determined to push Ferrari and Porsche from the LeMans Winner's Circle, developed one of the most successful racing efforts in history, beginning with the GT40s and continuing with the MkIIs. It gave Ford and Goodyear supremacy at LeMans.

A lot of things began to happen, seemingly all at once: The Shelby-Ford-LeMans alliance with Goodyears on Cobra, GT40, and MkII works entries; Dan Gurney getting the company involved with Jack Brabham in Formula I, and the late Richie Ginther introducing Goodyear to BRM, which resulted in direct tests against the formidable Dunlop operation.

In a way, Ginther might be credited with firmly planting Goodyear in Formula I racing. In the 1965 Mexican Grand Prix in Mexico City, Ginther started on the inside of the second row in a Honda. On Goodyears. In front of him were Jimmy Clark, on the pole in a Lotus, and Dan Gurney in a Brabham.

Race day proved very hot but Goodyear had done its homework. Their tires worked so well that Ginther charged into the lead on the first

Goodyear's plant at Wolverhampton, England, (top).

Richie Ginther, above, brought Goodyear its first Formula I victory.

Kay Campbell, 1966 Sebring Sweetheart and a Jantzen girl, after viewing the race from Goodyear's Mayflower, *followed by Peter Herbert of Alitalia Airlines.*

Left: Richie Ginther at 1965 Mexican GP; (top) 1966 Sebring, l-r, Mr Figerio of Alitalia, Kay Campbell, Lloyd Ruby, Mary Ulmann, Ken Miles and Alec Ulmann, race promoter. Ruby and Miles drove Ford No 1 to win; (above) Sebring '67 Start; (below)Gurney takes a turn at LeMans 1966; (bottom) a Ford pit stop at LeMans '66.

turn of the first lap. The freckle-faced Californian never looked back after the first lap. "I glanced in my mirror at the end of the first lap," he later recounted, "and didn't see a soul until I was clear past the end of the pits. I thought I must have dropped a gallon of oil and that they had all spun out behind me."

Ginther quickly built up a seven-second lead over Mike Spence's works Lotus before the Englishman succumbed to a strong challenge from Gurney's Brabham after eighteen laps. For the rest of the race Gurney threw everything he had into a strong counter-attack, but the Honda V-12 was clearly superior to the Climax V-8. In addition to that, Ginther wasn't making any errors. He drove smoothly and quickly, much to the annoyance of the European racers.

He roared around the track at 11,000 rpms, reserving the maximum of 12,000 revs in case he needed it. He didn't. He piloted his Honda to the Victory Circle as if he was off for a Sunday drive. Gurney's Goodyear-clad Brabham was second. It was Goodyear's and Honda's first Formula I win, and to say it whetted their appetites for more would be an understatement.

Following the Mexican victory, Goodyear persuaded former world champion Jack Brabham to test some new tires. Black Jack, so-called by his ever-present five o'clock shadow, was so impressed that he signed on with the Wingfoot clan. It was one of the great milestones in Goodyear's racing history because the remarkable Brabham won another Formula I World Championship in 1966. It was his second and Goodyear's first. Goodyear again won the championship in 1967 with Denny Hulme driving a Brabham.

When the larger three-liter engine formula was introduced to Grand Prix racing, Dunlop dropped out, leaving it all to Firestone and Goodyear, who both had superior carcass designs, compared to the exiting English company. It wasn't long before it became apparent that Goodyear would eventually have it all to themselves. It was a thought that company engineers didn't speak of, but one that the European press often theorized.

Goodyear's brilliant performance in international racing—winning the Formula I championship in 1966 and 1967 and winning LeMans

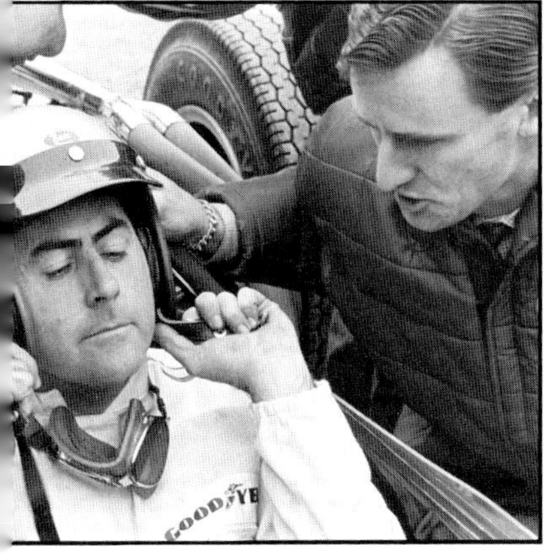

Formula I champion Jack Brabham prepares for yet another race, 1966.

LeMans '66, above left, a close finish between the Ford GTs of Hulme/ McLaren (left) and Amon/ Miles.

Targa Florio 1967: Bernard Cahier (left) and Jean-Claude Killy after winning 1st in GT class in their 911 Porsche, on Goodyears.

Denny Hulme, USGP, Watkins Glen, driving towards 1967 World Championship.

three years in a row—could be traced to an amazingly small number of engineers, with DeVinney leading the technical offensive and former LeMans participant (from his pre-Goodyear days) Fred Gamble handling the tactical front.

While DeVinney occupied himself with out-designing the competition, Gamble managed strategy in Europe, South Africa, Australia, New Zealand, Mexico and Japan. And the young engineer, Leo Mehl, emerged as Goodyear's compounding wizard.

The record speaks for the effectiveness with which the job was done. It wasn't exactly a David and Goliath scenario, but it was close.

One significant story surfaced during the 1967 Targa Florio, although it was quite by accident:

For the open road race (forty-seven miles per lap) in the mountains of Sicily, Goodyear's p.r. manager for European racing, Bernard Cahier and world champion skier Jean-Claude Killy teamed up to drive a works 911 Porsche "just for kicks." And maybe a little publicity. Nothing more.

Porsche agreed to this car running on Goodyear tires as the two amateurs posed no threat to their other two cars with professional drivers on Dunlops.

Goodyear, of course, assumed that Cahier and Killy would drive conservatively but, just to protect their hides, they mounted some special tires with the stickiest Formula I compound they could find. Just in case the amateurs got in trouble. The compound gave them a forty second to one minute advantage per lap over the factory-equipped Dunlop Porsches. With but one tire change for the 1,000 kilometer race, Cahier and Killy went on to win the under two-liter GT category, easily defeating the frantically hard-driven works cars. There were a lot of red faces in the Porsche camp. And some explaining that had to be done.

So, for those wide and wild sticky gumballs enthusiasts enjoyed from then on, there were a lot of pioneers to thank: Cahier and Killy, the young Goodyear engineers, the good ol' boys of NASCAR the SCCA sports car crowd, Jack Brabham, the California hot-rodders, the European racers and the Americans.

And don't forget that service station recapper and tire groover in Fort Lauderdale, Florida.

On the NASCAR Front

If the European racing front seemed to be frantic, the racing scene at home put it on the trailer. The classic Goodyear/Firestone battle on NASCAR tracks was far from a skirmish; it was full-fledged warfare.

Denny Hulme, left, and Leo Mehl beam over Goodyear's victory in the 1968 Italian Grand Prix at Monza.

To the right, Leo Mehl on left, then Goodyear's European racing manager, chats with Jack Brabham in England in 1968.

Goodyear Blue Streaks won one battle; Brand X won the next.

Race drivers have never been reluctant to jump on any band wagon that was going fast and, quite frankly, there were many days when even the most loyal Goodyear drivers showed up at the track using the tires with gold bands around them. It depended entirely upon who had the fastest tire that day, and as much as many of them would like to have remained loyal, their prime objective was to win the race. No matter what it took.

As Johnny Rutherford so aptly put it: "Some days you eat the bear and some days the bear eats you."

What had begun as a stock tire affair in NASCAR had rapidly evolved into one of the most bitter battles in the annals of motorsports. Both companies were spending literally millions of dollars on tire design and compounding. They came up with new carcass designs, new compounds and new tread patterns. Week after week. And then they worked on various combinations of these factors. All in all, there were dozens of types of tires at each tire test. And, needless to say there was a fair amount of corporate espionage involved.

As one tire company tested, there were people from the other camp in the stands, masquerading as fans, who had binoculars trained on precisely what the engineers and technicians were doing in the pits. They also paid strict attention to where the tires were stored because there were more than a few midnight invasions of the garage areas. They climbed fences and did, in general, anything they could to get their hands on one of the "new" test tires. It was like a Mexican border crossing. There was as much activity in the garage area at midnight as there was at noon. Sometimes more.

If either company was successful in "borrowing" a sample of a new tire, they took it back to Akron to dissect it and to see why it worked. Or why it didn't work.

It became so obvious on most mornings that there had been visitors during the night that Goodyear began "planting" tires in easily-obtained places, just so they would be whisked away to Akron. They were marked in chalk "O.K.!" These "plants," of course, were not test tires at all, but ones that had been made to look like race tires that were no more than wider versions of passenger car tires.

Firestone caught on quickly and did the same thing. This brought about spies in the pits during tests—men, sometimes drivers, who kept a keen eye on lap times and where the "good ones" were hidden away.

There were times when the drivers helped Goodyear's effort to keep secret their best test tires. On one particular Daytona test, Richard Petty had been warned that some of "his buddies" who were watching might be Firestone informers, so Richard went out on a set of "control tires"—ones they used as a gauge for the new compound and tread design tires.

1966 Goodyear Blue Streak Sports Car Special.

Goodyear's Sports Car Special for 1968 had a very different tread pattern than the 1966 model above.

The entire Goodyear crew is pictured following A.J. Foyt and Dan Gurney's great victory in the 1967 24 Hours of LeMans.

When he came back, he said loudly, "Man, these are the best tires I've driven in a long time."

The engineers were amazed, because they thought the tires weren't worth a damn competitively. In fact, they had put them on the car as a benchmark for the better tires. It wasn't until Petty got engineer Ed Long's attention that he winked at him, letting him know that the tires were not all he had said they were. Richard got a bonus in his testing paycheck that time.

The next day one of the tires was mysteriously missing. And when

An employee at the Wolverhampton, England, plant hand carves a rain tire in the late Sixties.

Goodyear Board Chairman Russell DeYoung, center, discusses tires at Daytona in 1960 with Lee Petty, left, and Big Bill France, the man who brought NASCAR racing to the forefront.

race day came, Firestone showed up with a tire that was more than a mile an hour slower than the Goodyears.

But, with Rutherford's words of wisdom, Firestone later did the same thing, using Bobby Marshman as their decoy.

The guys in red won the next race.

All is fair in racing and war. And this was both.

Tire Life

Here's an example of how informal things were in the stock car circles of the early Sixties:

"Jim Early, who was my boss, wanted me to go to a stock car race," says Mehl. "I had never been to one, so we decided to go to Atlanta. The race had been rained out a couple of weeks before but all of the cars had qualified so all they had to do was line up and run the race.

"We went down there on a Saturday night and before I went to my room, I asked Jim what time to meet him for breakfast at the hotel dining room. 'Breakfast,?' he asked. 'Breakfast. Hell, we don't have time for breakfast. We'll have to leave here by five o'clock in the morning.'

"When I asked why in the hell we had to leave at five, he replied, 'Well, the race is at twelve-thirty and we have to air all the tires.'

"Here I was a tire compounder from Akron and I had to *air* tires," Mehl says. "But I was ready at five. It was June 29, 1963, and by the time we got to the track, the sun was just starting to come up. It also was starting to get hot.

"Jim said, 'This has been a really good practice and qualifying for us; we've got a good tire—thirty-three of the forty-four cars in the race are ours.' And then he said, 'Tire pressure is very critical so *we* have to check the pressure in every tire.' "

Mehl made some calculations: Thirty-three cars, plus four tires each, plus back-up tires, maybe ten sets each; Early was right, they needed to be there by daylight.

"You start at that end of the pits and I'll start at this one," Early told Mehl. So off they went, unstacking tires, checking pressures and restacking them. After an hour or so, Mehl asked, "Wouldn't it be easier if the crews did this?"

"No," said Early, "We're engineers. This is our job."

Somehow Mehl imagined an "engineer" to be more of, well, an engineer. Not so in those primitive days. An engineer was *every*thing. By about ten-thirty, they were done. The temperature was already ninety degrees and the humidity was close to one hundred percent. "I was exhausted and it was still two hours before race time," Mehl remembers.

Early gave Mehl further instructions: "When the race starts, you take the end of the pits you worked on and I'll take the other."

"What do I do?" Mehl asked.

"When they come in they'll change right side tires; they won't change the left ones because it'll take too much time," he said. "So you should go over the wall [it was legal in those days for a tire rep to be over the wall] and get a treadwear reading on the left side tires, because they're going to ask you if the lefts will make it to the second pit stop."

And then Early added a statement that really opened Mehl's eyes: "It's your responsibility; if they blow a left side tire, they're really gonna' be mad."

Mehl had figured which drivers he was responsible for—Richard Petty, Fireball Roberts, David Pearson and a bunch of other top-notch racers. He sure didn't want any of those guys "mad at him."

Formula I champion, Jackie Stewart, right, goes over the specs for a new Goodyear racing tire with a tire engineer.

Cale Yarborough, one of Goodyear's most staunch supporters in Sixties NASCAR action. (opposite page, top)

The master himself, Smokey Yunick, gets his race car ready for the National 400 at Charlotte in 1963.

Paul Goldsmith, right, and Goodyear Racing Field Manager Chuck Blanchard examine the cooler used in the "air conditioned" driving suit Goodyear developed.

While he was working on his list, one of the crew members came to him, wanting to know, "How long you think the right side tires are going to last?"

Mehl was startled, but he replied with the only answer he could come up with on short notice. And not knowing a damn thing about it: "Well, I figure you can go about eighty miles on a tank of gas, so the tires should last that long."

"That's funny," the guy said, "we were only gettin' fifty miles on them in practice, and that was before it rained for a week and washed all the rubber off the track."

"Hold on," he told the guy, and he went running to Early. "How long are the right sides going to last?" he blurted out. "One of the guys said we're only going to get about fifty miles out of them."

"Yeah, I guess that's right," said Early. "Maybe sixty."

"What do you mean, you *guess*?" he asked in panic. "What should I tell this guy?"

"There's no use telling him anything," Early said. "If you tell any of them to stop at fifty miles, they won't do it anyway. They're racers."

"Well, what *do* I tell him," Mehl persisted.

"Tell him to pit when Junior hits the wall."

"What?" Mehl screamed. "Whatta' ya mean, pit when Junior hits the wall? And who the hell's *Junior*?"

Early looked straight into Mehl's eyes and said: "Damn, Leo, Junior *Johnson*. Everybody watches him, and they know he'll just keep running full bore until he blows a tire and hits the wall. And then everybody will come in and pit, and we'll know how long the tires will last between stops in racing conditions. They do it all the time."

"I went to college for this?" Mehl muttered as he walked away, shaking his head.

When the race started, Junior's white Chevy took an early lead. He was going like the wind and, sure enough, at about sixty miles, BLOOEY! Junior blew a right front. He scraped the wall, gathered it up and headed for the pits. Everybody else followed him.

Mehl knew that stock car racing had a long way to go in terms of technology. So did everybody else.

Marque Wars

There is little doubt that Jim Reed's victory in the 1959 Southern 500 at Darlington had set racing fever loose in Akron—and in case you didn't know, that's a highly infectious little bug. Goodyear was elated with its win in the greatest stock car race of the time; Firestone was deflated with its apparent loss of a strangle-hold on a major form of motorsports competition.

Over the years, both companies got closer and closer to war. By the early Sixties it was there. So, too, were the car wars. Chrysler, General Motors and Ford each had found out that stock car racing sold cars. It had elevated Pontiac, for example, from the image of a "little old lady's car" to one of speed and endurance.

Fireball Roberts had as much to do with Pontiac's new image as anyone. Junior Johnson had done the same thing for Chevrolet and Richard Petty and Paul Goldsmith were doing it for Plymouth. As for Ford, there was Curtis Turner and Freddy Lorenzen and a host of drivers out there every Sunday driving their hearts out for Dearborn U.

The 1962 Daytona Speed Week was a perfect example: Not only did Fireball score a grand slam but he streaked to a new record speed,

Leo Mehl, center, and workers at the Goodyear Wolverhampton, England, plant compare a 1968 Formula I tire with that of a Morris Mini Minor.

Tony Webner, racing general manager, and Lee and Richard Petty look at a Goodyear test tire in 1960.

regardless of the distance, every time out. Six record-breaking victories, extending from the early February time trials to the drop of the checkered flag in the July 4th Firecracker event. And, in winning the 500, he carved his name into auto racing history as the first man ever to win a 500-mile race at an average speed of over 150 miles per hour.

Pontiac sales went up across America.

But, one by one, the factories began to drop out. The cost of developing new engines and sleeker bodies had become prohibitive to some. It wasn't as simple as building, say, a dozen race cars and sending them into battle. NASCAR would not allow any car or any part that wasn't available to the general public to be used on the race track.

Chrysler was a perfect example. Their "hemi" engine—which stood for hemispherical combustion chamber—became the terror of the tracks by the mid-Sixties. So much so that Chevy had already gotten out and Ford was threatening.

The infighting between Ford and Chrysler had started long before

In 1964 Bay Darnell became the first driver to put a race car in Lake Lloyd in the infield at Daytona. A retaining wall prevented future aquatic journeys.

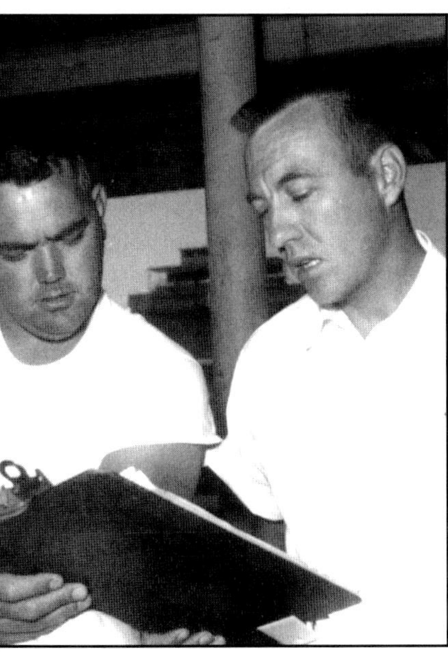

Junior Johnson, left, and Bobby Isaac compare qualifying speeds for the National 400 at Charlotte in 1963.

NASCAR favorite David Pearson at Daytona in 1962.

the 1964 season ended. Ford demanded of Bill France that their overhead-cam engine be allowed for 1965, Chrysler insisted that everything remain the same. So France called officials of the two companies together and, after several days of haggling, it was apparent that there was not going to be any amicable solution to the factory battle.

If France allowed the overhead-cam engine of Ford, Chrysler would go back to the drawing board and come up with an even more exotic power plant than their hemi. And all of racing would be even farther from the "stock" configuration. After all, France reasoned, there must be a certain number of the engines available to the general motoring public before they can be legal for racing.

Ford, meanwhile, said they would not compete in 1965 if the rules remained the same. Chrysler countered by saying *they* wouldn't compete if the rules were changed to allow the new Ford engine. It was like a Mexican stand-off.

France met again with industry officials, this time in Detroit, but the outcome was the more of the same. Ford said they must have the single-overhead-cam engine. Chrysler said that if Ford got that, then they would come out with the same thing, except that theirs would be a *double*-overhead-cam version.

The meetings and hassles that followed for the next couple of months were unprecedented. The general public got involved. There were arguments on every street corner in the Southeast.

Before that, nobody had any idea as to how important stock car racing was to the general public. The result was that France banned the hemi in the small Belvedere model because it was not available to the public in that form. Chrysler pulled out of racing. There was an uproar among MoPar fans.

Bob Anderson, Chrysler's vice president, expressed the fact that, "Racing has always prided itself on being progressive, and here we are now, backing up. Way back."

At Ford, Leo Beebe, head of special vehicles, said, "NASCAR is to be congratulated for its efforts to speed progress."

The outcome for 1965 was predictable. Ford ran away with everything. Track promoters screamed. Fans screamed. And a lot of them stayed home on Sundays, completely boycotting racing.

The problem was eventually worked out for the following season, but it had opened even wider the eyes of tire-makers.

This sport really *did* sell products. It was particularly important to Goodyear because a few years earlier, they had the same image as Pontiac. If one were to look in any parking lot, the hot cars or the custom ones displayed Firestones. Goodyears were found as original equipment on Chrysler products and on cars in shopping centers and country clubs.

Racing, after all, was an image-builder, and any company that was successful in it automatically assumed the "vital" image that appealed to the youth market—the segment of the driving population that spent the most money on their vehicles.

The picture was changing. The "baby-boomers" were there.

Within the few short years Goodyear had been back in racing, the breakdown was about even between Goodyear and Firestone tires on the hot rods in the parking lots and on the hot and custom street machines.

Goodyear workers, from the board level to the guy in the plant, took great pride in their racing rubber. Company publications banner-headlined important victories. National ads pointed to the success of the Wingfoot-equipped machines.

A. J. Foyt: Winner of the Indianapolis 500. Co-winner with Dan Gurney at Le Mans. The 1967 U.S.A.C. Champion. His tires: Goodyear Blue Streak racing tires.

Dan Gurney: Foyt's teammate at Le Mans. And first American in 46 years to win a Grand Prix r (Belgium) in an American car. His tires: Good Blue Streak racing tires.

The Big 4

s Hulme: 1967 World Champion. Winner of aco and German Grands Prix. Winner of 3 of 6 Am Races in McClaren cars. His tires: Goodyear Streak racing tires.

Jack Brabham: Winner of the French and Canadian Grands Prix. 1966 World Champion. His Brabham-Repco cars were awarded Manufacturer's Trophy for 1967. His tires: Goodyear Blue Streak racing tires.

Racing had begun to catch on as fans crowded the Charlotte Motor Speedway in 1963. However, modern facilities were far behind.

There was not to be a repeat of the 1921 fiasco, when Goodyear pulled out of racing because they had "proved the technological leadership of their cord tires and there was nothing left to prove."

Suddenly there *was* something to prove: A vital company image. Of course, they told shareholders that their tremendous racing budget sold tires and that the gap was widening between themselves and second-place Firestone in the marketplace—and it was. But the bottom line was that everybody liked to see the Wingfoot in the Winner's Circle.

Goodyear was there to stay.

Freddy Lorenzen, the Golden Boy of racing, proudly points to a record speed in qualifying for the 1963 National 400 at Charlotte. Lorenzen was driving a Goodyear-shod Holman and Moody Ford.

The mountain comes to Goodyear, in the form of two legends, Richard Petty and A.J. Foyt

Goodyear was riding high in NASCAR, and the great success of Richard Petty had a lot to do with it. Richard had been loyal to the company that had used him in so many stock tire tests. And using the young North Carolina driver had been a wise decision; not only was he proving to the racing world that he was someday to become a legend, he had proven himself the most popular driver on the circuit.

No person in the history of the sport, including Bill France, Sr., had more to do with its enormous popularity than Petty. He was its greatest salesman, simply because he let his presence be available to people, nearly twenty-four hours a day. This presence was noticed by all. It's almost like a friend who shows up when a loved one has passed away. It's not necessary to say a word: just being there is enough. This sort of presence was nearly forgotten in sports; it was confined to a boxing ring in Las Vegas, Nevada or a football stadium or New York's Madison Square Garden basketball court. But Richard's presence went out of the asphalt lanes of *his* playing field, right to the people.

And his association with Goodyear was carried right along.

Richard never made a single excuse for himself or in any way showed the slightest hint of arrogance. In fact, he may be the last of the Thirties-type sports heroes we'll ever have. In case you don't remember, the Thirties sports hero was anything but flamboyant; he simply went out there and broke records and then he sat down with the crowd and joked and talked.

Richard was far from flamboyant—nearly emotionless, if you want to know the truth—but he captured the hearts of more race fans than any driver who ever lived. Perhaps even in the "if it feels good do it" society of the Sixties, the vast number of Americans still believed in God, family and country; perhaps it sounds corny, but just maybe we don't hear from this silent majority. What Goodyear had in Richard as one of its spokesmen was a different kind of hero—the return of the all-American boy. Jack Armstrong hadn't left us at all. For all those years he had been alive and well in Level Cross, North Carolina.

Through it all, Richard was stock car racing's greatest ambassador. In the Sixties, stock car racing needed a shiny-toothed hero with roots strongly in the South to vault this sport to the forefront.

As great as Cale Yarborough was and as wonderful as Fireball Roberts and Junior Johnson were behind the steering wheel, it was Richard Petty who first got to the fans.

So it was easy to see why Goodyear used him as both a test driver and an ambassador. Petty was the first driver they thought of when it came time to test a revolutionary safety tire, one that would become so well-accepted that it would be ruled mandatory on every superspeedway in NASCAR.

Joe Hawkes, who was a quiet, unassuming engineer for the company, had an obsession. Unlike his racing engineer counterparts who mostly were gregarious, Hawkes worked, almost unnoticed, on a tire that would bring Goodyear NASCAR's top award of excellence.

There had been a period in the Sixties when six top drivers were killed, mostly from tire-related problems—either from tires wearing through or running over some foreign object on the track—sending the car into the concrete wall. Hawkes borrowed the principle of the Goodyear Double Eagle passenger car tire, which was a tire-within-a-tire. The precept was that if the outer tire failed, the inner one would carry the car safely to a service station, where it could be changed. This was a relatively simple procedure at highway speeds, but at speeds over 150 miles per hour, the concept would have to be fine-tuned.

"Racing improves the breed" is an axiom often advanced by manufacturers involved in the sport. But in the case of the safety shield air container—commonly called the inner liner—the breed actually improved racing.

The tire-within-a-tire idea that Hawkes improved upon for racing was of some concern to the racing division people. It was one thing to think of this on a Cadillac at, say, sixty miles per hour, but to put it on a near two-ton race car at nearly three times that speed was something else. But race drivers are a vigorous breed, so when Goodyear contacted Richard Petty and Darel Dieringer to test the tires at Daytona, they said, "Why not?"

"Maybe you guys don't understand," said engineer Ed Long. "We want you to run over some sharp metal spikes at race speeds and blow out the outer tire, just to see if the inner tire will keep the car stable."

"Sure, why not?" they again replied.

When Petty showed up with his familiar blue, Number 43 Plymouth and Dieringer with his red and black, Number 16 Mercury, everything was ready. They had taken pieces of two-inch pipe and cut them off about two inches long, sharpening points on the end that would slash away the outer tire.

Lifeguard Safety Shield in stock car tire.

Richard Petty pauses to examine four tires during 1965 Goodyear tire tests at the Daytona International Speedway. The tires were purposely slashed and punctured at high speeds while he tested a new safety concept in racing tires—an inner tire which remained inflated.

Stock Car Special, 1965, above; and the 1966 model below. Note tread pattern differences.

One of the critical problems was to come up with the proper length of the pipe, so that it only damaged the outer tire and didn't get to the inner one. It wasn't exactly the most scientific test ever done, but the drivers had a lot of faith in Goodyear. And, the engineers, in turn, had a great amount of faith in the mild-mannered Hawkes.

Dieringer was the first driver out. He hit the piece of metal at 150 miles per hour, with the nonchalance of a taxi driver. The outer tire didn't blow. So he came back around the tri-oval and hit it at 165 miles per hour. There was a slight noise and Dieringer felt the right front tire "thump." But he maintained control of the car and brought it safely into the pits.

The engineers placed some more spikes on the track and Petty climbed in his car, buckled up and said to Dieringer, "Ain't this some way to make a livin'?"

Dieringer agreed that there might be safer ways, but neither of them would have changed their occupations for any amount of money. Racing was a dangerous sport and if this new idea of Goodyear's would save lives, they were more than willing to go along with the company's belief.

It was both a tribute to their driving skill and courage and a vote of confidence for Goodyear.

Petty's right front outer tire blew the first time he hit the sharp object on the back straightaway—at about 170 miles an hour. The car

Darel Dieringer sits on a Blue Streak Stock Car Special prior to the 1964 Nashville race. Dieringer, along with Petty, tested Goodyear's inner shield safety tire.

bobbled slightly as it entered Turn Three, but he gathered it skillfully up and came roaring into the pits.

"Okay, boys, you've made a believer out of me," Richard said. "Let's do it again."

Goodyear had introduced the greatest safety device in the history of racing. No longer did a blown tire necessarily mean that a car was going to crash into the wall. The new concept gave them a "second chance."

Later that year, NASCAR mandated that all racing tires on superspeedways must be equipped with the inner liners. Goodyear eagerly passed their technological knowledge on the tire to Firestone. Beating their cross-town rivals was one thing, but to save even one life was another.

Indianapolis: De Ja Vu

As the Goodyear racing picture began to unfold in the South and in Europe, there had begun a great rumble in the Midwest. The hottest driver on the United States Auto Club (USAC) circuit started it; Goodyear followed suit, because it would lead them to the world's premier race.

A simple but terse telephone call that came from a phone booth somewhere within the confines of the Indianapolis Motor Speedway's fabled Gasoline Alley on May 9, 1963 proved to be the icing on a very large cake.

A.J. Foyt, Indy racing's fierce and fiery hero, had won the race two years before on Firestones. The tire part wasn't unusual. *Every* driver had won the Indy 500 on Firestones since Goodyear turned its back on the Indiana oval four decades earlier because that's the only choice the drivers had. That race was what seemed to keep Firestone fired up. And each year a double page ad appeared in *The Saturday Evening Post* and all the other magazines of the period, showing a small photo of every car and driver that had won the race on their tires. It impressed almost everyone. The exceptions were Goodyear's racing people. And Anthony Joseph Foyt, Jr.

The truth is, Foyt was madder than a wet hen at Firestone. Smokey Yunick had designed and built a lightweight Indy racer and it was running so well that Foyt was convinced that Firestone had given Yunick special tires. To complicate things even more, Colin Chapman had showed up with a rear-engined Lotus Ford and, with Jimmy Clark at the controls, it, too, was outrunning the traditional front-engined, Offenhauser-powered roadsters. Firestone said they hadn't given either car special tires.

Foyt was not convinced, so he stomped to the telephone and called Goodyear in Akron. "Why don't you guys bring some of your Stock Car Specials down here?" he said. "We can show these Firestone guys something."

There was no doubt that Goodyear would have gotten to Indianapolis again within a few years; it was in their plans. But Foyt's phone call started the wheels rolling a whole lot sooner. When they called Foyt back to tell him that they were "thinking seriously" about taking him up on his plan, Foyt was elated. For one thing, they had listened to him.

The tires used on Indy cars traditionally had been tall, skinny and hard. They were compounded to carry the heavy front-engined roadsters around the Indy track safely and for relatively long distances. There had been precious little change in them for years because there was no reason to change much. They were the only game in town.

The tires Goodyear brought to the track for Foyt and any of the other drivers so inclined to try them, were much lower in profile, wider and of a softer compound. But, unfortunately, they had been designed for cars that weighed twice as much and they simply didn't work well enough on the roadsters. They didn't get enough "bite," so Goodyear elected to go on back to Akron. Before they loaded up their tires, Goodyear promised Foyt that they would be back, right after the race, with some new tires to test for the 1964 race. And they assured him that he would be their Number One tester. They wanted to make sure they kept him in their camp. After all, he was probably the best Indy driver of all time, so they considered themselves lucky to have him on their side.

It was surely one of the wisest decisions they had ever made. Parnelli Jones won the race that year; Clark was second, Foyt was third.

All on Firestones.

And the double page ad ran once more.

But, back in Akron, the midnight oil was burning. An all-out Indy tire program was being instrumented. They fully intended to live up to their promise to the burly Texan.

One Step at a Time—Indy

The old garages with the double wooden doors in Gasoline Alley at Indianapolis were part of the tradition of the age-old racing facility. It was where the original Nationals and Duesenbergs and Millers sat, waiting for their attack on the "brickyard." They had housed the finest race cars in the world.

The bricks were the only things that had changed over the years at Indy. And the cars. The primitive cars had been replaced with a succession of Miller Specials—turned Offenhausers. First there was the lay-down engine that allowed the car-builders to lower the profile of the car and make it less wind-resistant, consequently faster, and then there were all of the engine and suspension improvements that made them quicker. And safer. The drivers and car-builders had finally attached roll bars and seat belts and the drivers wore much safer helmets. The sport had improved, but tradition still reigned at Indy. Absolutely nothing about running the race had changed. It was Grant Wood at speed. There could easily have been an "American Gothic" racing team.

The garages had seen all of the changes—except a few that had burned just before the start of the 1941 race. But the burned garages were rebuilt, exactly as they had been. And it was in one of these garages that Goodyear's current Indianapolis history began—one that was to be as renowned as anything anybody had ever accomplished there, including Firestone and their skinny tires and double page ads.

The day the first Goodyear test tires arrived in June of 1963, it was raining. It was one of those wind-driven Midwest rains that comes from one direction for awhile and then the other. And then straight down. It lasts for hours, until rivulets run in all directions. It usually is accompanied by a gloomy, listless fog that floats a dozen feet off the ground, bestowing the sinister mood of an old Charlie Chan movie.

Several of the Goodyear engineers sat in the garage and talked about the rain and what they were going to do that night. Jim Loulan was there; so were Ed Alexander and Ed Long. All engineers. None versed even in Indianapolis talk, let alone Indy savvy.

A.J. Foyt was there. He said very little because he didn't know the Goodyear guys very well and Foyt simply doesn't bother with small talk with anybody he hasn't known for a long time.

He answered some of the questions—the ones that he considered worthy of an answer. To some of the "small talk" questions he merely nodded a response; others, too absurd to be distinguished with an answer, brought about a slight trace of a smile. A.J.'s smile is disarming; it has been known to paralyze full-grown women at twenty paces. Or it can bring an end to a conversation he feels is going nowhere.

The tough Texan rose, walked to the back of the garage and placed his hands on either side of the engine cowling of the pearl-white Sheraton-Thompson Special. In that light he looked a lot like a preacher about to begin his sermon. But his would not put anyone to sleep.

"Where do we start?" he asked.

The engineers looked at each other and then at Foyt. Where the hell *do* you start when you're locking horns with a company that had been there, in full command, for five decades?

Where do you begin to move mountains? Well, first of all, you listen to the guy who brought the only shovel. So Foyt began his sermon in earnest. He began to tell the tire experts what it was all about—this Indy 500—and what Firestone had done wrong and how it could be corrected.

What he said made sense to the engineers, who were taking notes as the "boss" spoke. And Foyt was the boss. He was Captain Marvel. Superman. And Goodyear knew damn well that they were fortunate to have such a man as not only their advisor, but their friend. It was the one constant to which they could plot their course.

A.J. told them the story of how he had won the 1961 race, which still is one of his favorite tales:

"Eddie Sachs was on the pole in the Dean Van Lines Special that I had driven in my first and second Indy races (1958 and 1959). Don Branson and Jim Hurtubise were beside him. In the second row were Rodger Ward, Parnelli Jones and Dick Rathmann. Those were the six cars I had to pass to get out front. It couldn't have been much tougher, but that's what makes Indy the race it is. If it was easy, nobody would give a damn about it; it's like trying to catch that big bass that's been in your favorite fishing hole for years. If it was easy, the fish wouldn't still be there."

Tony Bettenhausen had befriended Foyt when he came to Indy as a brash kid. He was one of the few race drivers Foyt ever idolized, but A.J. had sat on the pit wall during a practice session earlier that May and watched Bettenhausen die in a terrible, grinding crash.

"When I got to the track on race morning, I could still see the skid

Tire engineer Ed Alexander compares four Goodyear passenger tires with 1968 Speedway Specials.

marks and I remembered watching Tony's car spinning and flipping. That kind of thing bothers a race driver, but nobody ever talks about it. You just talk that much more about how you're going to win and about how much faster you're going to go.

"On the start, Hurtubise jumped out in front of Sachs and Branson. I tried to move up but it was hard to do because the cars in front of me were as fast as mine and the drivers were good, so I waited for my chance."

There were two crashes and a few engine failures in the early stages of the race that left Parnelli Jones in the lead. To give you some idea how tough drivers were in those days, listen to this:

A piece of metal on the track was thrown up from a car Jones was about to lap. It hit him right above his goggles. Jones was bleeding so badly that his goggles filled up with blood. He emptied them three times and would have kept on doing it if his engine hadn't blown.

Parnelli Jones is perhaps the only driver as tough as A.J. Foyt. They both had big, barrel chests and arms that looked like those of a stevedore. If they had ever gotten into a fight, they would have torn up concrete for blocks around.

But with Jones out of the race, Foyt passed Sachs for the lead. It surprised everybody, including Foyt.

"I couldn't believe the feeling. I was leading the Indianapolis 500. But with less than two hundred miles to go, Sachs got by me. He was using up most of the 'groove,' so I got down on the apron, almost in the grass, and I went past *him*."

The crowd was going wild with first Foyt leading and then Sachs. They traded the lead ten times in the next one hundred miles.

"When you're out front in a race and there's somebody chasin' you real hard," Foyt said, "you hear all kinds of noises from your car. You hear rattles that were never there before, and you feel vibrations you never felt in your life. You're sure everything is falling off your car. But I had a car that was built by George Bignotti and I was sure it would hold up for 500 miles.

"I began to get paranoid. I thought every car I passed was going to run into me, and I thought every car I pulled up behind was about to spin. Hell, I got to thinking that something was going to come out of the bushes and get me."

Courage and skill alone will not necessarily win a race. It takes teamwork, and both Foyt and Sachs were going to have to pit once more. The tires and fuel on neither car would go the distance. What happened in the pits could make the difference.

Sachs went in first. Exactly twenty seconds later he was out of the pits with new tires and fuel. Foyt had a commanding lead, but he hadn't pitted. Two laps later he got the message on the pit board one of his crew members was holding at the edge of the pit wall: "Pit 2." It meant he had to come in two laps later. He took a deep breath.

"I was going to give up the lead to Sachs, but what made it worse is that I wondered if I could ever catch him again. After all, his pit stop had been a good one."

Foyt slid sideways as he got to his pit because he had come in so hot. He pounded the steering wheel with the butts of both hands and he yelled at the crew. Eighteen seconds later, the car went back down on the track and he felt Bignotti pound him on top of his helmet.

"Eighteen seconds! Man, I had a chance. I saw Sachs go past me as I roared back on the track. Two laps later, I was right on his tail again. I couldn't believe it, I was actually gaining on him more than I had at any time in the race. I sailed past him, and as I did, I glanced over and I saw his teeth clenched; I have never seen such a look of determination on anybody's face. But I knew he couldn't pass me."

Sachs stayed right on Foyt's tail but he didn't have quite enough speed to get past.

"I had the race won. The Indy 500. That's what I thought, but I hadn't any more than gotten the thought in my mind when I saw my pit guy with the board. It said 'Fuel low!' How the hell could the fuel be low, I was just in there?

"The next pit sign said, 'Stay there,' and I knew that they must be working on whatever had gone wrong. Somehow I knew I was running out of fuel; that's why I was faster than Sachs's car: I was lighter. I found out later that the fueling hose wasn't working right and they had only gotten half a tank in."

Two laps later, the sign Foyt feared most went up: "Pit A.J." He swallowed hard and got ready to come back to the pits.

"There were tears in my eyes when I came roaring down pit road. They put in a splash of fuel, just enough to finish the race, and I was out in eight seconds. There were fifteen laps to go. I got within sight of Sachs and I drove deeper and deeper into the turns with each lap. I was right on the ragged edge. Eddie was too because he wanted to win as much as I did.

"There were four laps to go when I felt the vibration. It wasn't the car. It was the crowd. You can *feel* it. You don't hear it; you feel it on your skin. You can feel it when a crowd is standing and screaming. There were 300,000 people screaming. I knew something had happened to Sachs. I knew I had won. I knew it."

When Foyt came around, he saw Sachs's car in the pits. The right side was up in the air and they were changing the right front tire. The old Firestones had a layer of white rubber beneath the tread rubber, as a warning to let drivers know if they had run the tire into the danger zone. At the speeds Sachs was running, trying to keep in front of Foyt's lighter car and later trying to catch him, he had worn the tire down to the white. Also the extra fuel load had made his tires wear faster than Foyt's.

"It must have been the toughest decision of his life," Foyt told the Goodyear engineers, who all were silent and wide-eyed. "If he had stayed out there the last four laps, he would have won. But if the tire had let go, he would have crashed and at those speeds there's a good chance he woulda' been killed."

Foyt won the race by eight seconds. The question for the next two or three years was: "What would you have done in Sachs's place?" Al Dean, Sachs's car owner, said he would have stayed out there. Clint Brawner, Foyt's car owner, said he would have stayed out there. Sachs said he would rather finish second than finish dead. It was Jim Loulan who asked Foyt, "What would *you* have done if you were in Sachs's place?"

Foyt thought for a few seconds because nobody had ever asked *him* the question. He got a very serious look on his face: "A man's life is the most important thing in the world to him. Is any race worth going that far out for—I mean, far enough to look over the edge? Even the Indianapolis 500?"

And then there was a glint in his eye.

"I would have stayed out there."

Goodyear decided at Indy they were going for the lead; they wanted Firestone chasing them.

It's tough to push around a company the size of Firestone—particularly one that had more experience in racing than anybody—and say "Excuse me, fellows, I want to play, too." Unless you've got a *very* good product.

One thing in Goodyear's favor was that it was considerably larger than Firestone, so they could spend the money necessary to make a "very good product." And spend it they did, although after the first few days of testing it became painfully apparent that it was going to take a lot more money than they had thought. For one thing, they needed more field representatives, since the company was becoming involved in more types of racing; they hired Chuck Blanchard and moved Ted Lobinger into racing full-time. And they placed Chuck Kerns full-time within the plant to supervise the building of race tires.

The testing procedure they used was much the same as they had done earlier at Riverside with Dan Gurney and Graham Hill in Formula I tests. It worked like this:

They mounted the control tires—which were ones that they felt were a "happy medium" in handling and wear—and then they ran two or three sets of test tires. Sometimes four. Somewhere along the way, without the driver's knowledge, they put the control tires back on. That way they could look at the comparative speeds and get his unbiased comments.

The control tires also were used to establish which drivers were able to detect a real difference in compounds and construction. A lot of great race drivers are not great testers.

A.J. Foyt chats with engineers at the first Goodyear tire tests at Indianapolis in 1963.

A.J. Foyt did not fall into that category. He could detect the control tires on the first lap. In fact, he could tell more about a tire's handling in two laps than most drivers could in half a day.

"The first batch of test tires they showed up with at Indy wasn't much better than the stock car tires they had brought down before the race, but we had to start somewhere," says Foyt. "I took the roadster out and tested tire after tire, telling them each time what I thought this tire needed and what particular synthetic compound felt best, what stuck better in the turns or broke loose or whatever."

Foyt's word became law to the engineers because he proved to be one of the best tire-testers in the business. For one thing, Foyt is a master mechanic. There wasn't a nut or a bolt or a suspension part or valve spring that he hadn't either installed himself or had overseen the installation. He knew exactly what his race car was capable of and he could quickly distinguish the difference between an ill-handling tire and a race car that wasn't quite set up right.

Goodyear used a number of other drivers for testing, as well. Johnny Rutherford, Lloyd Ruby, Roger McCluskey, Don Branson, Bobby Unser, Jim Hurtubise and Gordon Johncock were some of the early ones hired and they gave good tests, but not being as directly involved in the mechanics of the race car as Foyt, there were times when they weren't quite sure if the car was set up badly or the tires were slower than the ones they had tested before.

Johncock, however, was so talented that he could drive on almost anything. Goodyear used him as the final tester. They figured that if it would last thirty or forty laps on his car it would last that long on anybody's. Rutherford also could get out there and run consistently fast laps, and this proved valuable to the engineers because they could get good heat readings, and he gave extremely reliable regularity and durability tests. He did exactly what he was told.

"Foyt was unique," says Mike Babich, who was administrative assistant to Tony Webner. He also was the scheduler and orderer and deliverer and picker-upper and everything else for the Racing Division. "If we asked A.J. to go out and run a set of test tires ten laps, he might run them five or one. He could quickly tell whether or not they were what they needed. Or he might stay out there twenty laps if he felt he needed more time to evaluate one particularly good set against another.

"Foyt was a master at tire-testing. For one thing, it was impossible for 'spies' to tell what the Goodyear tires were doing when he was driving because he never ran a lap at what we called full speed. So nobody knew what he had or what was going on. He'd have somebody timing him through [Turn] Two and he'd go as fast as he could there. And then he'd slow down. Next lap he'd have somebody in Three and then Four and so on. So when he put the times all together, he knew what we had. Firestone didn't.

"There were times when he came in after a lap and said 'Jack some more weight on the right front,' or the right rear. Or he'd immediately say, 'This tire's good' or 'This one isn't worth a damn,' " Babich recalls. "He mixed it up and, in so doing, mixed up the guys in the grandstands with the stop watches."

It was difficult to pick out spies because at Indianapolis every time somebody starts a race car engine, five hundred or so people miraculously appear in the stands in Turn One. It was easy for the Firestone guys to blend in. Except from Foyt, who, even at race speeds, could pick out anybody he knew.

Here's a perfect example: One testing day, Parnelli Jones stood in the pits, watching as Foyt circled the track at near record speeds, particularly in Turn One. He turned to Goodyear's p.r. guy and said, "Let's go over in Turn One and watch Foyt come through the corner."

Why not? What better way to find out how A.J. looks than to have Parnelli as an observer. But when they got there, sitting in the middle of the five hundred fans, Parnelli revealed his real reason for wanting to go there. "Watch me get Foyt in trouble," he said.

"Whatta'ya mean, *get Foyt in trouble*?"

"Well," said Parnelli, "I know when he's going to be the busiest, so I'm going to wave to him. He'll be afraid I'll think he's a chicken if he doesn't wave back."

Foyt had not yet come around and the p.r. guy was sure A.J. wouldn't pick them out in the midst of the crowd, in spite of the fact that Parnelli had on a red Firestone jacket and he had on a blue Goodyear one; there were jackets of all colors in the stands—Foyt wouldn't see them. *Wrong.*

As Foyt approached the turn, full bore, Parnelli waited until exactly the moment when he knew Foyt was the most involved in trying to keep the car in its proper line through the corner. And then he raised his arm high in the air and waved it back and forth. He was right; there was no way Foyt was going to let Parnelli get the best of him. Foyt's right hand shot up in the air briefly in a half-hearted wave. The race car bobbled and it looked for one frightening second as if he might lose it, but the

Johnny Rutherford tested tires for Goodyear for a number of years. Here Rutherford discusses the Gulf-Mirage performance with John Horsman, left, managing director of Gulf Research Racing, after trying the sports car for the first time during tire tests at Watkins Glen in 1973.

master "gathered it up," and sped into the short straightaway that connects Turn One with Turn Two. You just *knew* he was grinning.

"Damn, Parnelli, what'd you do that for anyway?" Goodyear's man sputtered.

"I just wanted to see how Tex's reflexes were holding up," he said, with the Cheshire Cat grin that's known so well.

Even when Foyt wasn't in the car he was right there in the pits to help the engineers. For example, Don Branson was out there running fast laps and one of the engineers said, "Man, he's runnin' good." Foyt said, "Sure, but just listen to the tires in the corners." You could hear them screaming. "You're gettin' good speeds but he's workin' twice as hard to get that speed, which really doesn't tell you what you want to know. Just don't show them the pit board and see what happens," he said.

They tried it, and the speeds went down. Branson—and the other guys, for that matter—were trying to beat their own times. It's a temptation race drivers can't resist.

"They're not trying just to go fast and feel the tires," Foyt said. "What you need is for the guy to run consistently faster speeds, and not be working harder and harder to do it. That'll tell you which tires work best and not which driver."

Engineers and Espionage

"The big advantage we had over our competition was that our engineers didn't stop with design and compounds," says Leo Mehl. "They very quickly became conversant with what it took to make a

Ed Alexander, left, and Ed Long, center, chat with Eddie Sachs during Goodyear's early tire tests at Indianapolis in 1963.

uniform tire—and uniformity was the key, we learned."

The bias-ply tires in the mid-Fifties were made out of rubber and nylon, both of which are highly susceptible to temperature. It's not like the materials that came along later which could be controlled.

In those days, it even depended on how hard you left the pits as to what size the tire was going to grow. They found out that they could compensate this by "stagger." They actually staggered the tires from right side to left side in size so that what might upset the handling of the car due to an even slight difference in size might be partially corrected.

"The dimensions of the tire were absolutely critical. At Indy, for example, we found that a perfect arc in Turn One is if the right rear tire is .18 inches bigger than the left rear tire," Mehl revealed. "We also found that one pound of air would make a difference of several hundredths in size, so the drivers and engineers began to talk in terms of a twenty-five stagger or a thirty stagger. What they were talking about was the difference between .25 inches or .30 inches, which represents several sheets of typing paper."

The handling of a car, they found, could be altered dramatically if they put on a tire that was .05 inches different in diameter.

A whole new world of terminology was being created. Not to mention an even larger world of technology—trial-and-error technology at first, but more and more scientific with each day of race tire testing.

Goodyear was not alone in tire advancement. The minute Goodyear finished its two weeks of testing, Firestone moved in. "I'll bet it was the first serious testing those guys had done at Indianapolis in twenty years," says Foyt.

As Firestone tested, there were a few guys in the grandstands in Turn One with Alan Ladd-type hats pulled down over their eyes, watching every move that was made in the pits and on the track.

When Firestone moved out, Goodyear moved back in, with a fresh batch of test tires. The tire war definitely had spread to the Midwest.

If a Goodyear tire blew, all the engineers tried to pick up every little piece. They didn't want a shred of evidence left behind that Firestone could take back to Akron and analyze. They had a crew just to watch tires and pick up pieces. Clarence Cagle, who was in charge of maintenance, thought the Goodyear guys were the neatest people who had been to the speedway in years.

"We kept all the pieces from Firestone," said Ed Long, "but then we realized we were losing whole tires. No matter how much security we had. Somebody in our organization was making them available to Firestone. We never did find out who it was, but we countered by finding a source for Firestone tires. It would have been easier if we just said, 'Okay, fellows, let's just trade. That way we can let about ten guards and six sweepers go.' But we didn't. That would have taken away all the intrigue.

"Besides, what we found out from their tires led us to believe that we were gaining on them. We worked late at night, getting the cars all set up for the next day, and there was always a run to the airport to get a new batch of tires that had been made that day in Akron. There were many times when the tires were still hot when we unloaded them from the airplane. They actually had twenty-four hour shifts running in the Akron racing tire plant. I'll say this for them: They were dedicated to the huge job they had ahead of them."

After the late-night work sessions, the engineers met to analyze all the findings from that day's tire tests. There were many days when they went straight from the meetings to the track to begin testing again.

The spies didn't get much sleep either.

But was Firestone really the benchmark for Goodyear? "I suppose so," Mehl ventured. "Knowing what your competition is using and duplicating it isn't a bad way to go, but once you get competitive then in the long run, as far as racing goes, it's not really the thing to do. The reason is that you spend all your time getting where they are, and by the time you get even with them technically, they've moved ahead.

"It finally dawned on us that even if we absolutely, totally duplicated our competition, we were only equal with them. We hadn't really proved anything, so we decided that we were going to go for the lead. We wanted them chasing us."

Goodyear decided right then and there that they wanted to be the Daddy Rabbit.

Speedway Special

When all testing was done and both Foyt and Goodyear were convinced that they had the tire to do the job, production on the new Speedway Special tire began in late 1963, in preparation for the 1964 USAC Championship Car season. Foyt ran the tires with some success in the early races. In fact he won the season opener at Phoenix, Arizona, which gave Goodyear its first Indy car victory in decades. By the first of May, the Wingfoot crew was ready to tackle the "big one"—the Indianapolis 500. It had been four decades since a Wingfoot tire had been there, and even then, there hadn't even remotely been the amount of preparation as there had been for this one.

There had been some question whether or not there was any relativity at all between racing and passenger car tires, but, as it turned out, the engineers had found at least two things: Materials development—tread and carcass compounds and fabric materials—and molding techniques, which further developed the low profile race and passenger car tire.

"We learned a lot of molding techniques in the early days of racing that later came into the performance tire," says Walt DeVinney. "Reverse molding was one. It worked like this: We had a contour in the mold that was reversed—it dipped in the center, which is exactly the opposite of what it would be when it was inflated, but by doing this, we were able to keep a flatter tread and keep the wide bias-ply tread on the ground.

"Earlier molds had a flat contour so when the tires were inflated, the tread became rounded instead of flat. This reverse molding had a dramatic effect on a tire's handling characteristics. Before that, we had to keep building up the shoulder with more and more rubber, to keep the tread flat; this, of course, caused heat build-up in that area and tended to cause the tires to chunk. With the new molding design, we felt we were ready."

So, too, was Firestone, as it turned out.

Growing Pains

The White Front Restaurant and Bar in Speedway City offered a free meal each day to the driver who had the fastest practice time for the Indianapolis 500. It became a great psychological battle between Goodyear and Firestone, and also between Foyt and Parnelli Jones. Every day between five and six in the evening it was a two-man race, but it was a lot like boxers psyching out the other guy, staring him down before the main event.

This "free meal" was costing the companies thousands of dollars each day to win it. Foyt told Goodyear what was happening with the tires and they called back to Akron for some modified ones for the next day's battle. So did Firestone. Goodyear had a system: They called by nine o'clock each night and the compounders and tire-builders had the new tires on a plane to Indianapolis the next morning.

By Friday, Foyt and Jones seemed to be equally fast. Qualifying the next day would determine the pole position and give whatever company who pulled it off a tremendous psychological boost.

But on Friday morning, Parnelli again rolled out "Calhoun," the name he had given his Number 98 Offy roadster. There were no rules about fuel then, but there seemed to be an unusually strong odor coming from Parnelli's exhaust. It didn't matter because there was an odd smell about Foyt's exhaust fumes as well. He would never tell anyone what he added to his fuel when he really wanted to go fast, but it smelled a lot like shoe polish. Everybody figured the odor was there to mask what was really boosting horsepower.

Everybody at pitside knew it was going to be a monumental day. The outcome was far beyond anybody's wildest dreams. They took Parnelli's car back to the garage, closed the doors and began working on it, and by midafternoon, he took the car out again and he went more than five miles per hour faster than any speed Foyt was able to muster.

They returned the car to the garage once more, covered it and closed the doors. Foyt went crazy; he went back to the track and he drove so aggressively that he had the car sideways in the turns. He did everything he could, coming close to crashing several times, but he could not get even near Parnelli's speed.

"Every time A.J. came in, there was a different story," recalls Mehl. "He said 'the tires vibrate,' or 'they're junk.' He was madder than hell."

Nobody knew how Parnelli had done it, but by the end of the day Firestone's head of racing, Bill McCrary, came to Foyt and said, "If you're going to win this race, you're going to have to put some Firestones on."

Foyt pondered the issue. Goodyear had been loyal to him and he had been loyal to them. The thirteen other drivers who were running Goodyears awaited Foyt's decision. He was the pivotal point in Goodyear's entire Indy program.

On Saturday morning, Foyt rolled his car out on Goodyears. It appeared to all that he was going to qualify them. He wore a uniform with a prominent "Goodyear" on the left side, high enough that photographers had to catch it in close shots.

After several attempts to reach Parnelli's speed, Foyt brought the car to the pits and it was pushed to his garage. He sat behind closed doors and discussed the situation with the Goodyear guys.

"Look, A.J., you're our boy," someone said. "You've gotten us this far, but the most important thing for you is to win the race. You do what you have to do. We'll understand."

Foyt looked at each of them as they left the garage and closed the doors. With a loyalty that was as fierce as his driving skills, Foyt wanted to stick with Goodyear, but he also had a feeling that he could win his second Indy 500 that year.

Time passed. Everybody waited. By noon, the garage doors were opened. Foyt's Number 2 roadster was pushed out toward the track—on four fresh Firestone tires. As he walked past the Goodyear engineers, he looked at them and shrugged his shoulders. The look they gave him was one of respect. It said, "It's okay, partner, we understand."

By qualifying time all fourteen cars that had been on Goodyears were now on Firestones.

The double page ad was virtually assured for another year.

Jimmy Clark got the pole position. With him on the front row were Bobby Marshman and Rodger Ward. Parnelli was fourth and Foyt was fifth. They were the only two front-engined cars that anybody thought

A.J. Foyt roars to a record 200.4 mph in 1963, setting a Closed Circuit Speed Record at Goodyear's San Angelo, Texas, test track.

had a chance against the faster and better-handling new rear-engined creations. In fact, those front-engined cars already were being referred to as dinosaurs.

Before the race Parnelli said to Foyt, "We might just have to run over a car or two, if we expect to win."

"Well, buddy boy," Foyt replied, "if those guys in their funny cars can't keep ahead, we might just have to do that."

Eddie Sachs was driving a rear-engined car. He was starting in the middle of the sixth row, right behind Davey MacDonald, who was driving one of Mickey Thompson's cars. Davey had said he was concerned because the car didn't feel just right but most dismissed it because he was really a sports car driver and they just assumed he hadn't gotten the *feel* of the speedway yet.

"If you get in trouble here," MacDonald said, "there's no place to go. All these walls, you know."

Foyt needled Sachs before the race: "That's the guy you're followin' out there today, Eddie."

As they lined up the twenty-seven Firestone-equipped cars for the start, there was a difference about one uniform. A.J. Foyt wore his Goodyear driving suit. It was his way of saying "thanks guys," for the close association he had with Goodyear.

When they dropped the green flag, Parnelli and Foyt shot past Ward and closed the door on Dan Gurney who had also started to move up. Clark took the lead going into Turn One and Marshman tucked in behind him. Jones and Foyt were single file behind the two lead cars. They stayed that way for the first lap—a freight train with two new diesel engines and two old steam locomotives right behind them.

None of the lead cars even saw what happened behind them. MacDonald came out of Turn Four and hit the bump in the track that the veterans knew had been there for years. The car got sideways and spun into the concrete retaining wall on the inside of the track. It bounced off the wall and the fuel tank split open, spreading fuel all over the track. It exploded. Sachs couldn't see anything but flames as he came roaring into Four. He T-boned MacDonald's car. Sachs's fuel tanks broke open and a wall of flame shot up into the air. It was like a hydrogen bomb had been dropped. Ronnie Duman drove through the flames to safety, Johnny Rutherford's car went through the flames and sailed right over what was left of MacDonald's car, and it landed on all four wheels on the other side. He kept going.

The red light that means "all cars stop," came on. It was only the second time in Indianapolis history that had happened. The other drivers stopped in Turn Three and got out of their cars, watching in silence as the flames reached higher and higher. Some of them walked away because they didn't really want confirmed what they already knew. Sachs's and MacDonald's cars were right in the middle of the flames.

Foyt remembered what Sachs had told him after the 1961 race: "I try not to think about it too much. It just screws me up. That's how much I want to win. I think of Indianapolis every day of the year, every hour of the day. When I'm sleeping, I dream about winning it."

Sachs had been in the hospital fifteen times from crashes, but when friends admonished him with, "Why don't you quit, you're going to kill yourself," he replied "Well, quitting would be like dying to me, so..."

When the flames were extinguished, there was nothing left of the Sachs and MacDonald cars but charred skeletons of once proud racing machines. Track attendants draped tarpaulins over the cars before they were removed from the track.

After about an hour, an announcement was made. It was highly unusual, but everybody knew what had happened. The statement began: "Ladies and gentlemen, it is with extreme sadness that we make this announcement..."

The great crowd-pleaser Eddie Sachs and the rookie Davey MacDonald were dead.

There were seven cars missing from the field when they restarted the race nearly two hours after the accident. The drivers tried to dial it out of their minds. It's something they must do. Foyt thought of how fast Clark's and Marshman's cars were and he knew how tough Parnelli would be to beat. He tried to put it all out of his mind by planning his strategy for the rest of the race.

As the race wore on, Marshman went down below the line in Turn One and bottomed out, knocking the plug out of his oil pan. Clark, who had come to the race with Dunlop tires on his British car, found out what Goodyear had learned: It's not that easy to conquer the Indy track. His tires began to come apart in big chunks. So did Gurney's Dunlops, on the other Lotus Ford. Colin Chapman called them in.

Suddenly it was Jones and Foyt. In the dinosaurs. Nobody could run with them. When Parnelli's car caught fire in the pits, it was all over.

The day belonged to Foyt.

As Foyt pulled into Victory Lane, the cameras clicked and clicked, each one showing the tough Texan with a bottle of milk in his hand, a wreath about his neck and "Goodyear" emblazoned across the left side of his uniform. As the ceremonies went on, Raymond Firestone presented Foyt with a check for $7,500—the contingency money for winning the race on Firestones.

Foyt gave the check back to him.

All's Fair in Racing

It was two years before anybody found out why Parnelli's car had gone so fast on that final day of practice, and it came about when Johnny

Pauleson, who had been a mechanic on the Jones car, went to work for Foyt. In a motel room at Indianapolis, Pauleson confessed to Mehl how

J.A. Loulan inspects X-ray equipment that will tell him if Goodyear's newest racing tire, the Speedway Special, is ready for competition. The unique inspection step was adopted by Goodyear to assure maximum quality in the tires for the 1964 Indianapolis 500.

they had done it.

"I always felt bad about what Firestone had done to you poor innocent Goodyear guys," he said.

Mehl knew it wasn't the tires, so he asked him, "Okay, how'd you do it?"

"Well [Bill] McCrary came to me before the season and he said, 'You know Goodyear is coming, and they've got a tremendous tire, and I'll have to tell you, we're concerned about it. What I want you to do is build a big engine. It'll only have to run two or three laps because we'll probably run fifty percent nitro in it."

Nitromethane, which is an additive that was allowed, boosts the horsepower but large amounts of it will cause an engine to literally explode if run too many laps.

McCrary told Pauleson he would pay for the engine and that if they had to use it and it worked, there would be a bonus in it for him. Pauleson built the engine.

"So when all else failed,Pauleson said," "we put the engine in. It

worked. After the super run, we pulled the engine out of the car and nobody ever saw it again." Pauleson, who was later killed in a light plane crash, said that both he and Parnelli Jones were paid five thousand dollars that night.

Firestone hadn't done a thing illegal. They hadn't tried to qualify or even race the big engine. They broke no rules. The whole exercise was designed to totally demoralize the Goodyear drivers, particularly Foyt.

It worked.

It cost Goodyear all fourteen cars they had.

Andy Granatelli talks with his driver, Bobby Unser, in the Hotel Tropicana Special at Indy in 1963. It was one of the very first Goodyear Indy tire tests.

The 1964 Speedway Special, shown below.

"For my next act, I'm going to set myself on fire."
—Craig Breedlove

You might say that Goodyear was up to its corporate ears in motorsports. In fact, you would *have* to say it. So it was difficult for them to turn their backs on a project as glamorous and exciting as the quest for the World Land Speed Record. The record hadn't been in the hands of the Americans since April 22, 1928, when Indianapolis hero Ray Keech sped across the sandy beach at Daytona at the remarkable speed of 207.552 miles per hour in his mighty White Triplex, powered by three Liberty aircraft engines mounted on a chassis made from steel railroad tracks.

After that a succession of Englishmen wrested away the title from each other; first it was Major H.O.D. Segrave who piloted his 1,000 horsepower *Sunbeam*, then Sir Malcolm Campbell came along with his 2,500 horsepower *Bluebird* and successfully raised the record, year after year, until he reached a speed of more than 276 miles per hour in 1935.

He determined that was the limit of the beach course and moved his traveling show to Utah's Bonneville Salt Flats where he stunned the world with the first 300-mile-per-hour run. The record stood until 1946 when John Cobb upped it to 394.2 mph.

The World Land Speed Record was all but forgotten for a number of years, until a bright-eyed teenager read about it in an encyclopedia at his school in California. Craig Breedlove, who had built his first hot rod when he was fourteen, stared off into space in his civics class that day. He decided right then and there that his goal in life was to bring the record back to the United States.

As Breedlove dreamed about the prospect, he remembered what President John F. Kennedy had said in his inaugural speech: "Ask not what your country can do for you; ask what you can do for your country." At the ripe old age of sixteen, Craig Breedlove, who finally had his driver's license and was racing his hot rod on weekends at the Muroc Dry Lakes in southern California, began making sketches of what his Land Speed Record car would look like. He even had a name for it—the *Spirit of America*.

Everyone who knew the boy agreed that when he planned, he planned big. They also agreed that someday he probably would accomplish his dream. As the years passed, Breedlove went from his original '34 Ford coupe to faster and faster cars. He became somewhat of a hot rod prodigy, breaking record after record. Along the way he built up an assortment of friends who could help him with his plans for the Salt Flats. One was a master model maker, who produced a perfect scale model of the car. It would have cost him a couple thousand dollars to simply go out and hire such a person to build a model, but this one was offered as a token of faith in the youthful racer's ability.

Another friend worked for Lockheed Aircraft and made it possible for Breedlove to test the model racer in the company's wind tunnel. Again on faith.

He was ready. The first step obviously was a sponsor, so Breedlove scraped up enough money for a coach airplane ticket to Akron, Ohio. He called and made an appointment with Tony Webner.

With the only shirt he had without writing on it and his only pair of dress slacks he arrived at Goodyear's doorstep, with the model under his arm. Everybody in Akron immediately liked the handsome youth. Here was another all-American boy.

Craig Breedlove was first a racer, but secondly he was one of the greatest salesmen of all time. Partly because of his enthusiasm and partly because of his obvious knowledge of his project, he wound up in the office of Goodyear's president, Victor Holt.

The sales pitch was honest and perfectly presented. At the end, he said, "I need the backing of the best company in the tire business; that's why I came to Goodyear."

Holt asked how much he needed. "Ten thousand dollars," he replied. "Plus land speed record tires, of course."

"Can we build tires that will go four hundred miles an hour?" Holt asked Jim Loulan, who had been brought into the meeting for his technical expertise.

"We can build them," Loulan said, "but I don't know if we can test them at that speed." And then he added, looking at the earnest look on the youth's face, "We can do it."

Breedlove left Akron with an advance on his ten thousand. He had made a similar arrangement with Shell Oil. Now he had the $20,000 he had estimated it would cost to build the *Spirit of America*, and he had tires and fuel.

In 1963 the dream came true as Breedlove sped across the Salt Flats in his jet-propelled, thirty-eight foot long racer at an average speed of 407.45 miles per hour and brought the Land Speed Record back to the United States after a long absence.

Walt Arfons stands beside the jet-powered Wingfoot Express *he designed and built for driver Tom Green, who established the World Land Speed Record of 412 mph in 1965. The record stood for only a few days before Breedlove came back to break it. Arfons then built an improved, rocket version of the* Express.

The rocket version of the Wingfoot Express *streaks across the salt at Bonneville.*

He toured the entire nation, appearing on local TV talk shows and radio shows, and getting his story and photo in almost every newspaper in the world. He was an instant hero.

South of Akron, another hot-rodder read it all with great interest. He was older than Breedlove, by twenty years. But he had tons of experience in building superfast cars. Art Arfons had worked over the winter of 1963-64 on his own jet creation, the *Green Monster*. He would run on Firestone tires.

In the meantime his brother, Walt Arfons, had made his own pitch to Goodyear. He, too, had a car powered by an aircraft jet engine. He wanted badly to beat his brother to the punch, so he went to Goodyear with his car. Walt's car looked good, but they didn't want to put as much in the car as they had in Breedlove's (the final cost figure was well into six figures).

The racing public relations manager came up with an idea: "If we call it the *Wingfoot Express* maybe we can get some ink out of it."

The company agreed to a limited sponsorship. Walt took the car along with driver Tom Green and went 413.20 miles per hour, which was good enough for the record.

But it wasn't good enough to deter Breedlove, who came back eleven days later and upped the mark to 468.719 mph.

All of a sudden, in a sport that the world thought was dead, there were record cars everywhere.

Bobby Leppan stands behind the motorcycle designed by Alex Tremulis in 1965.

Crew members service the Cobra Daytona Coupe that set twenty-three endurance records at the Bonneville Salt Flats as Goodyear driver Bobby Tatroe dives from behind the wheel and co-driver Craig Breedlove (right) prepares to take over during a brief pit stop. The car averaged 150.095 miles for twelve grueling hours, traveling the entire 1,802 miles on one set of Goodyear racing tires.

The Daytona Coupe in action at the Salt Flats in 1965.

Craig Breedlove and two crew members look at all that remains in sight of the 38-foot Spirit of America *after a terrifying crash at more than 500 miles per hour on the Bonneville Salt Flats in 1965.*

Breedlove, wanting to become the first man to travel more than 500 miles per hour, as well as being first to set the over-400 mark, came back two days after his 468-mile-per-hour run and went well over 500 on his first attempt. To officially establish a record, a car had to run through a measured mile one way and then, within one hour, had to repeat it the other way. The average of the two runs was his official time, which was recorded by USAC.

Breedlove was a little nervous as they topped off his tank with jet fuel. He checked the tires and the aluminum skin. There were a few slight buckles in it from the tremendous wind pressure at such high speeds, but the car looked fine to him. He climbed into the cockpit of the three-wheel creation and fastened his safety harness. As he pulled on his helmet, he gave the thumbs up sign and his crew clamped on the canopy.

A few minutes later, Breedlove was off in a roar. As he approached the measured mile, there was a giant rooster tail of salt billowing up behind the *Spirit*. But when he entered the measured mile, the car began to veer off to the right. He knew that he wouldn't go between the timing lights, so he backed off the throttle. The car came back to the center of the black line that guided him across the snow white salt course.

He knew there was something wrong with the steering, so the second he was past the timing lights, he hit the button on the steering wheel that deployed the drag chute. The speed was too great for the chute and it tore loose. He looked at the brake pedal. He knew that the aircraft disc brakes were designed to slow the car from about 150 miles per hour. He was still traveling across the salt at 500.

"I didn't have any choice," he later said. "I pushed the pedal. It went right to the floor. I knew the brakes had burned out instantly," Breedlove said. "Here I was hurtling along at 500 miles an hour with no steering, no chute and no brakes. I figured I was in trouble."

Breedlove also was a master of understatement. There was a five mile build-up, the measured mile and five miles to stop the car. At 500 miles an hour, the car covered a mile every seven seconds. The south end of the course was coming up fast.

"I was at the end of the course with the press cadre, where we expected him to come to a gradual stop," explains Goodyear's p.r. man. "He was still going 500. In an absolute gesture of futility, I ran for my high performance Mustang convertible. Even at 150 miles an hour I couldn't see where he had gone. I ran the car as far as it would go into the shallow water past the end of the course, maybe another four miles. I jumped out and began running, following the tracks in the mushy salt. The car was nowhere in sight. A huge drainage ditch had been built to drain the brine into a processing plant where the minerals were extracted. There was a twenty-foot-high salt dike as a result of the excavation for the thirty-foot-deep canal. The tire marks went up over the dike.

"Gasping for breath, I reached the top of the dike. I froze as I saw a small portion of the tail protruding from the briny water. I half slid and half tumbled down the other side and by the time I reached the edge of the water, Craig bobbed to the surface. I pulled him to shore and helped him get his helmet off. He looked at me and said, 'For my next act I'm going to set myself on fire.' "

Breedlove's account of the episode made newspapers and television stations all over the world:

"When everything had failed, I relaxed and looked around," he said. I focused on the inside of my goggles, and then I looked at all the instruments and I remembered putting every one of them in. I looked at

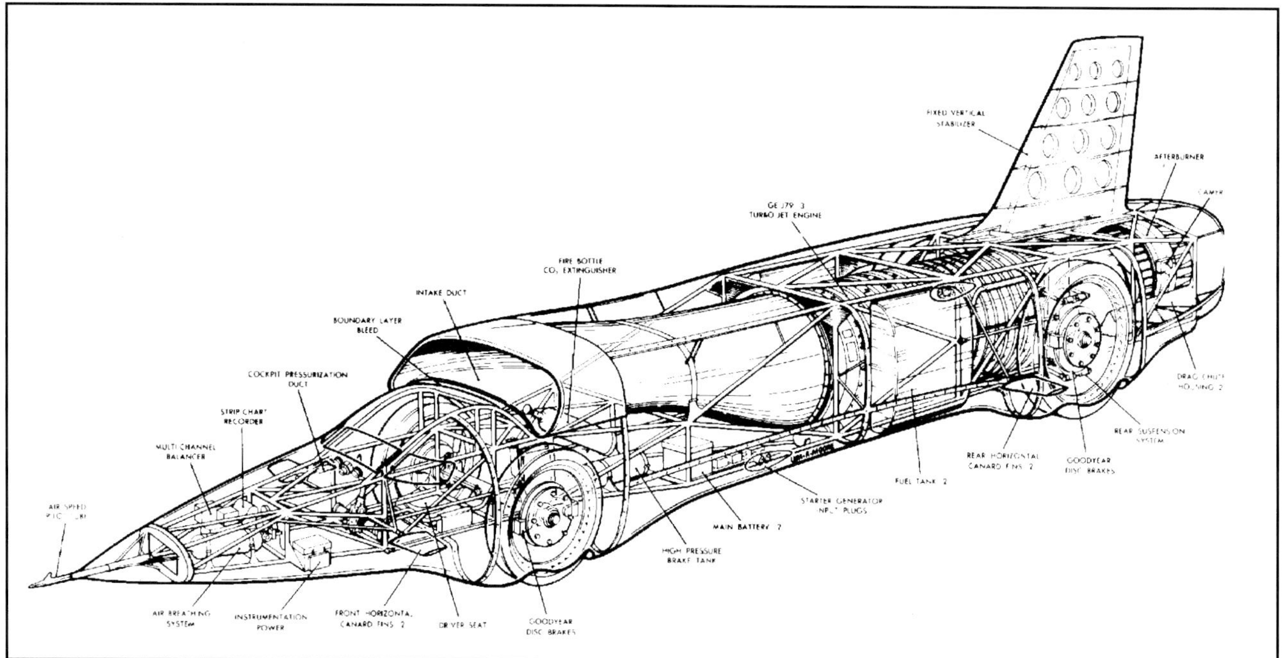

A cutaway drawing of the complexities of Craig Breedlove's Spirit of America, Sonic I *in 1965.*

the canopy and the roll cage, and I remembered making all the welds.

"And then the damnedest thought came to mind: I remembered what someone had said when his Indy race car was sliding sideways down the front straightaway at about 150 miles an hour: 'I thought about getting out, but I figured a man could get hurt at that speed.' I laughed out loud.

"As the car started up the dike I figured this was it, but when it reached the top, the right out-rigger fender dug into the salt slightly. It righted the car and I was flying. Straight. And quiet. Then it began to fall and as it headed for the water, I released the catches for the canopy because I knew that it was going to be impossible to get it off once the car was submerged.

"As the car began to sink, I unbuckled my safety harness. I tried to pull myself out, but I was stuck. I was underwater and I couldn't get out. I thought, 'Damn, all this and now I'm going to drown.' But then I realized what was holding me. I hadn't unhooked my oxygen mask. So I pulled it loose and floated out of the cockpit."

Breedlove was unhurt. He held the Land Speed Record at an average of 526.277 miles per hour. He still is listed in the *Guinness Book of Records* as the holder of the world's longest slide in a vehicle. Five miles. Just before the winter rains and snow came that would close the Salt Flats for six months, Art Arfons blazed across the course at 536.71. On Firestones.

The following year, Breedlove was back with a new, bigger and more powerful, four-wheeled car, the *Spirit of America, Sonic I.*

Craig Breedlove, below left, presents a model of his successful Spirit of America *World Land Speed Record car in 1964.*

Bobby Tatroe, left, and the Wingfoot Express *and Craig Breedlove, right, and the* Spirit of America, Sonic I *stand beside the two Goodyear-sponsored cars at the Bonneville Salt Flats in 1966. Walt Arfons, center, was the builder of the* Wingfoot Express.

A jubilant Craig Breedlove is hoisted to the shoulders of his crew after accomplishing the world's first 600-mile-per-hour run; 1966.

The beat went on.

Art Arfons crashed his car that season, also at a speed above 500 miles an hour, and walked away. Completely away.

After many attempts—each one nearing disaster—Craig Breedlove established a new record of 600.601 miles per hour. And he, too, walked away completely.

It had been the most dramatic period of Land Speed Record racing in its sixty year history. The first mark had been set in 1903 by millionaire car-builder Henry Winton—at 68.198 miles per hour, in a car he also had built himself.

Equality to All

"Sure money played a big part in helping get Goodyear to the top," says Mike Babich, "and we probably spent more money than they did, but we learned a lot of ways to save dollars that Firestone was losing in every race.

"They still weren't convinced that we were a serious threat at Indy, but they started a big prize program in stock car racing where a driver running their tires every race would get "X" number of dollars. If he ran more than two-thirds of the races on Firestones, he would get a bonus of about $100,000.

"We decided we didn't want to spend money that way. We'd beat them with our product. So race after race, more and more drivers began to get the message: To win, you had to go with Goodyear. Both Ford and Chrysler were breathing down the drivers' and car-owners' necks to win.

"About halfway through the season, Firestone realized that the drivers were getting restless," recalls Babich, "so they changed things; they said okay this week doesn't count against you, hoping that they

Goodyear's general manager of racing, Tony Webner, left, compares the tires of Indy great A.J. Foyt, center, and Craig Breedlove, World Land Speed Record holder.

would have a faster tire the next weekend, and sometimes they did."

Firestone knew a lot about tires, but Goodyear really broke their backs in stock car racing. Firestone had a lot of experience, but they simply got caught flat-footed. A perfect example is a 500-mile race at Atlanta. Freddy Lorenzen, one of the Holman-Moody Ford/Firestone's hot shoes, started the race on Firestones. It didn't take him long to see that the Goodyear-shod cars were outperforming him. What happened went unnoticed until Jim Foster, who now is president of the Daytona International Speedway but then was sports editor of the *Spartanburg Herald*, reported in his column that Lorenzen had a system worked out with his pit crew. It was before the days of two-way radios, so Lorenzen had a piece of chalk with which to write on his driver's window. As he came past the pits, the crew saw a big "G" scrawled on the window.

They hustled over to the Goodyear tire truck with four wheels and said, "Get us four tires. Quick!" Several laps later, Lorenzen came in and his crew bolted on the fresh Goodyears.

Lorenzen won the race.

Foster closed his column with this: "Ever try to write a 'G' backwards at 135 miles an hour?"

"There also was another thing going on across town that hurt them," Babich remembers. "They were giving certain drivers better tires than others. Sure, we had placed more emphasis on some teams, but that stopped in 1967 when we realized you couldn't do that. Every driver had to get the same tire and the same treatment as all the others had. It was the only fair thing to do.

"If a tire was designated D2501, every tire in every pile was exactly the same—with the exception of basic manufacturing tire variations in size, which, of course was slight. Besides, the drivers used this for stagger.

"So, you see," Babich points out, "it wasn't so much that we were outspending them, we were building a reputation for fairness. It was another example of the dedication and integrity of our people."

Foyt/Goodyear on the Pole

Meanwhile, back at the Brickyard, A.J. Foyt put on one of the greatest qualifying shows in Indy history. He had won the 1964 Firecracker 400 at Daytona on Goodyears in a Dodge and would repeat it in a Ford the following year, but here's his account of the 1965 Indy qualifying:

"I guess you could say I'm a flag-waver—strictly American. I wouldn't even drive foreign cars. Hell, I wouldn't even wear a shirt with French cuffs. It was only natural that when I got to Indianapolis in '65 and saw all the European cars there, it pissed me off. And the European drivers. I made up my mind right there that I was going to sit on the pole.

"First off, Mario Andretti—who was born in *Italy*—set a new track record of 158.849. There were about 100,000 people there to watch, just for *qualifying*—and they went wild. They always do when someone breaks a record. Or his ass.

"I was next in line, but I told the USAC officials that I had a problem with my injectors. I *said* that, but actually I was stalling. I wanted to see

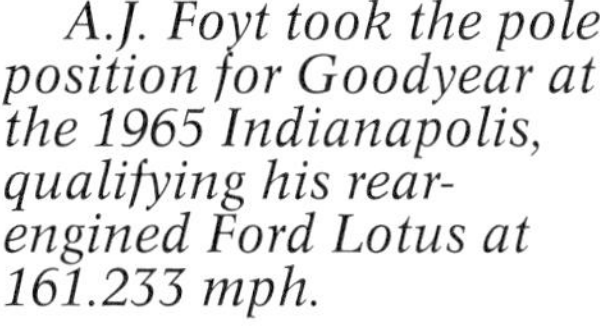
A.J. Foyt took the pole position for Goodyear at the 1965 Indianapolis, qualifying his rear-engined Ford Lotus at 161.233 mph.

how [the late] Jimmy Clark was going to do. He was British, you know. So my crew pushed the car back to the garage area. This automatically moved me to the end of the qualifying order, right behind Clark.

"Clark pushed the record up over 160," Foyt recalls, getting excited as he goes on. "I'll have to admit, I figured that was going to be hard to beat. The place was a madhouse. They still were screaming when they pushed my car back to the pit area. In fact, when they saw me coming, they let out a roar you could hear all the way to East St. Louis. "It was five minutes till six—five minutes till the track closed for qualifying. Five minutes left to get the pole. By the time the starter was in place in the nose of the car, it was fifty seconds until six. But all you have to do is get the car on the track *before* six; then you can stay there until you take your four qualifying laps. The engine started. Then it sputtered and died. Everybody in the place was on their feet. It started again and died. The third time it ran. They pushed me out of my pit and I was on the track with five seconds to spare. I hadn't intended to cut it that close."

Foyt is up on his feet now, gesturing wildly: "My first lap was 159.665. The second was over 160. The crowd had stopped screaming. They *all* were holding their breath. I was, too, because my car wasn't as fast as Clark's. I've never admitted it, but I was hanging it out so far that I was right on the edge of disaster in every corner. I was *over* the edge, if you really want to know, but I'll be damned if I was going to let some Brit beat me."

Foyt had five miles to go—two laps—and he needed to find half a mile an hour. The third lap was over 161—a *whole* mile an hour faster. His fourth lap was also over 161. When the announcement was made that he had a new track record of 161.233, everybody exhaled at the same time. They tore up programs and threw hats and just about tore down the speedway. When the announcer stuck the microphone in Foyt's face as his car came to a stop in the pits, A.J. said simply: "It's good to bring the record back to the United States."

Andretti didn't like it; Clark thought it was funny. But Foyt was on the pole. So was Goodyear.

Goodyear Perseveres—Indy

Everything was fine for Goodyear in qualifying. They had twelve cars in the race, which was an unbelievable effort for only their second

A.J. Foyt, right, and Craig Breedlove, take a break to talk with Goodyear's p.r. man, Bill Neely, in the Goodyear garage at Indianapolis in 1964. Foyt won his second of four Indy races the following day.

year. Everything was fine, that is, until "Carburetion Day," which is the Thursday before the race. It's another part of Indianapolis tradition. The cars didn't even have carburetors anymore, they had fuel injection, but still it was called "Carburetion Day." The fourth day of qualifying was behind them and this was the only time when the cars ran with a full fuel load. They had qualified with barely enough methanol for a couple of warm-up laps and four qualifying ones, just to keep down the weight and subsequently make the car go faster. Now the cars were heavier.

Much to the horror of Goodyear and the twelve drivers on the Speedway Specials, their tire treads began to come apart, throwing big chunks of rubber everywhere. They came in immediately and the engineers began to study the problem. Goodyear's p.r. guy hid under the Speedway grandstands.

USAC rules stated that a car must race with the same tires upon which it qualified, so there was no way Goodyear could change anything. They had to work with what they had.

"We found out that it was a blade wipe problem," explains Babich. "We had been able to develop shapes for the wider tires and shapes for the molds—we called them 'clamshell' presses. They went down like this," he says, as he places the heels of his hands together and touches the tips of his curled fingers on his right hand to the tips of the ones on his left. "The presses were hinged in the back and, in coming down like that because of their extra width, as opposed to coming straight down like a passenger car mold, blades in the mold 'wiped' the tread rubber and folded in the pre-cure paint.

"It would be just like taking bread dough and cutting it and putting butter in there to hold the layers together, but when you bake it, it's apt to come apart, when the heat builds up. We simply had too much rubber in the tread.

"We called Akron and had new tires built. Ernie Stadvec, who owned Shawnee Airlines, flew one of his planes down to Indianapolis the next morning with a batch of fresh tires," Babich says. "We took them out to the Winchester, Indiana, oval and ran them on a couple of the backup Indy cars that wouldn't be running in the race. We scuffed them down to the point where there was enough rubber worn off so that the heat build-up wouldn't be a problem."

The tires worked fine in the race, but Foyt's car went out with gearbox problems halfway through the 500. Jimmy Clark won the race. On Firestones. Even Foyt congratulated him.

Goodyear had nearly half the field in the 1966 race. They had twelve consecutive weeks of testing at Indy after the 1965 race. This time they weren't going to leave anything to chance. There were no tire problems at all, but on the first lap, rookie driver Billy Foster was pinched off and he spun into the outside wall on the front straightaway seconds after the green flag had been waved. Foster's car careened back across the track, starting a chain reaction crash that involved eighteen cars. Eleven of them, including Foyt, Gurney and a goodly number of Goodyear's other top drivers, were completely eliminated from the race.

It began to look as if Goodyear was never going to win the Indianapolis 500.

Nineteen sixty-seven was the year. Foyt started from fourth spot and all but dominated the event, winning by two laps and setting a new race record speed of 151.207 miles per hour. This time when Foyt was in Victory Lane with his Goodyear uniform, he also had four other things that were marked prominently with "Goodyear"—his tires.

It was the culmination of a battle that began with a phone call from

A.J. Foyt, following qualifying for the 1967 Indy 500, the year he won his third Indianapolis race.

Foyt in Victory Circle after winning the 1967 Indy 500. Foyt used the same four Goodyear tires while setting a record speed of 151.207 mph.

an irate A.J. Foyt in 1963, and was consummated with a checkered flag as his Number 14 rear-engined Ford blazed across the symbolic "Yard of Bricks" at the start/finish line.

The view from the top of the mountain was breathtaking to everybody from Goodyear.

After ten years of fierce competition, Firestone was gone. The "tire wars" had come to an end.

Things were happening fast. It seemed as if every month brought about a new challenge or a change of some sort for Goodyear's racing division.

Leo Mehl, the compounding wizard who had helped Goodyear win LeMans and Indianapolis, was sent to Europe in 1967 to manage the ever-expanding Formula I and sports car program. It proved to be a shift that would benefit the entire racing operation.

Even as Mehl packed his bags for the move across the Atlantic, Goodyear was becoming involved in drag racing, motorcycle racing, and the Sports Car Club of America's (SCCA) Trans-Am and Can-Am series. It appeared that with their great success in NASCAR and Indianapolis they didn't want a single form of motorsports to escape their watchful eye.

Tony Webner stepped down as general manager of racing and was replaced by Larry Truesdale, a Goodyear salesman from the Northeast who had been personally selected by Bob Lane, the public relations vice president. Since the racing division reported to public relations, the move was accepted.

Even with an inexperienced man at the helm of the racing division, it proved to be considerably easier to move into any form of racing in the Sixties and Seventies because everybody was doing something new; they were trying all sorts of innovations, but on a smaller scale than they would in the decades to follow.

Goodyear had a master plan, consequently it created a strong marketing and dealer organization. The company was fortunate to have as racing tire distributors, Carroll Shelby on the West Coast, Bob Schroeder in Dallas, Bill Robinson in Florida, Roger Penske in the Northeast and Ross Huggins in NASCAR.

"Because of the strong dealer organization, we had the nucleus to form a powerful marketing division, which controlled scheduling of the products for the field managers," says Mike Babich. "We had a field manager for stock car racing, two for sports cars, one for Indy and one for drag racing. These guys became experts and the racers knew that they could go to one man and get all the answers they needed. The other companies didn't have this kind of specialization."

The Goodyear racing program was run almost like an army. There was a staff meeting every Tuesday afternoon, after the field managers had returned from the battles on the various fronts. The field managers gave their reports and talked to the production people about what they needed for the next skirmish.

"Each area was like a battle unit," says Babich, "and if we went stock car racing, for example, we talked to the drivers and chief mechanics to see what problems, if any, they had. It was the same in any of the other things we were involved in."

Four-Wheelers to Two-Wheelers

The most unlikely place for Goodyear to end up was in motorcycle racing, because there was little interest within the company, all the way from Bill Still, who was manager of auto tire sales, to the board level. It wasn't their cup of tea.

"There was a lot of pressure from Harley-Davidson to get involved. They were racing and were a 100% Goodyear account for their street cycles. They wanted to race on American tires rather than rely on Dunlop or Avon who were regular suppliers to the English manufacturers, Triumph, BSA, Matchless, etc.

"We got pushed into it," Babich explains. "The Development Department first worked with Harley and when the program became viable we (Sales) were brought in to carry on the program. The early development was primarily done by Elmer Wasko." Babich continues, "Bike racing had been kind of a dirty word, but it was close to my heart so I was excited about it and agreed to take on the added responsibility.

"As was customary, we tried various ideas to improve the tires. One year we took some slicks to Daytona. We really had them there just for the drivers to see."

The drivers saw them all right. They asked: "What are those? You're going to groove them for dirt, right?" "No, no, no," replied Babich. "Those are your road racing tires for next year."

"A chorus of 'No way, man,' was the reply. "We're on two wheels remember and the rear is the most important one, so we're not going to run on slicks."

Babich assured them that the tires would work. The rest was relatively simple: They tried them and they loved them.

"The other tire companies were complacent," he says. "Dunlop, who almost had a lock on bike racing hadn't done much to change their tire. So we came in with a lot of good ideas. And a few bad ones."

Goodyear overcame the bad ones and thrived on the good ones. Motorcycle racing, as they say in the sport, was a whole 'nother ballgame. For example, the action on the high banks at Daytona was horrendous. Here were guys hurtling along through the turns at speeds equal to the mighty stock cars.

"Qualifying was done on the 2-1/2-mile oval—one warm-up and one flying timed lap—so we knew it was going to be fast," says Babich. "One fast lap and that was it. I went to Gene Romero, one of the top bike riders of the time, and said, 'let's try something different. For one lap you don't need a big tire, so if we use a smaller tire, we can reduce the rolling resistance.'

Motorcycle slick for road racing, 1973.

Action at Daytona, 1975. Gene Romero, 3, leads Steve McLaughlin, 83, through a turn.

"In those days, we ran a ribbed front and a diamond-tread rear. The rib was a 300 X 19 and the rear was a 350 X 19. They ran one warm-up lap and one timed one, so we put Gene out there with two fronts. He was one of the last qualifiers and he blew everybody off. It was too late for Dunlop to beat him. I think that caused everybody to really take a good look at Goodyear. We started to get the image of innovators, and bike racers liked that.

"Another time at Daytona, our front tire didn't seem to be adequate. It just wasn't big enough, so we decided to put one of the rears on the front. It worked great," Babich recollects. "It locked the front end, so they weren't washing out anymore. The interesting thing is that here we were with a tire that, according to the engineers, wasn't even shaped right, but it gave us just enough to do the job.

"The key to our success was expediency. We gave Dunlop fits. They were locked in with Triumph and BSA but, all of a sudden, we had a lot of drivers who switched to our tires, mainly because they liked our style. Gary Nixon was the first Triumph rider to switch."

"The program really got going when we got involved with Kenny Roberts," says Tim Miller, who now is area account manager of tire applications. "He was so talented that he caught a lot of people's attention. Bill Robinson, our distributor in Florida, was one. He took Kenny under his wing and he talked the development people into using him as a test rider."

Roberts was an instant success. He became to bikes what Richard Petty was to stock cars and A.J. Foyt was to Indy cars. After winning two successive championships in the United States, he and his team manager Kel Carruthers came to Goodyear about a European program. They had decided to take a crack at the world's championship in the 250cc class.

"They needed a bit of money, plus some help from Yamaha USA. Goodyear agreed to take a shot at it," says Miller. "The Europeans laughed at us. They just couldn't believe we would jump right in and take on Dunlop, Michelin and Pirelli, who had been around bike racing since Day One."

They obviously didn't know Goodyear. This was exactly the challenge that had taken them to the top in every form of racing they had ever entered.

"We went over there in 1978 and Kenny blew them away, in both 250 and 500cc classes," says Miller. "He won race after race, but toward

Goodyear motorcycle ribbed front tire, vintage 1965, at top, and diamond-tread rear tire used for motorcycles in 1966, above.

Kenny Roberts, right, in classic position at Daytona, 1975.

the end of the season he decided to concentrate on the 500cc class. He could have won the championship in both, but he chose to win big in 500cc. He won easily."

Roberts stunned the European motorcycle racing fraternity. Long before he had won three world championships in a row, the laughing had stopped. Kenny Roberts proved that he was the best there ever was.

"Nobody will ever know what percentage of victories were the tires and what was Kenny's ability. To the Europeans, here was this kid—the only one to have Goodyear tires, so they must be magical. It was a case where we were in an entirely new area; we had shot one bullet and it had hit the bull's eye.

"When Roberts got on a bike he was like a computer. He could tell what the front forks were doing or the back ones, the tires. Everything. He became a phenomenal tire tester. He went out there and ran a few laps and then came back and had them set the bike up exactly the way he wanted it. While his crew was doing that, he went out on the other one. He was the only one who could tell if it was the bike or the tires, and he never missed," marvels Miller.

"Because of Kenny we did a lot of construction changes and new mold designing. We took on new compounds and got highly specialized in motorcycle tires. The rears are so different from the fronts—the angle of attack—so basically the rears control everything on a bike. Kenny could tell us what to do, so if it was too soft, we went back a couple of notches and finally we had the right tire for that particular track.

"We had a low key program. The team carried the tires. I was the lone engineer, so I was the tire fitter, the tire designer, the p.r. man, the whole show. One minute I might be mounting tires and the next I might be on NBC Sportsworld, being interviewed by Paul Page. Then I went back to mounting tires. It wasn't as glamorous as it appeared," Miller continues.

"I'm not sure we would have had the success in bikes without Kenny. At one race he said, 'Hey, it looks like rain. We'd better carve out some rain tires,' so we got the grooving iron. Kenny drew a pattern on the slick tread surface with a pencil. It did rain and the design we had carved in the tread worked so well that it eventually led to directional tread tires.

Kenny Roberts rests between Goodyear tire tests in 1976.

Kenny Roberts, 3, moves into second place at a European world championship event.

Caught by the camera in mid-air at the 1978 Daytona 200, Kurt Lentz heads for the haybales.

A Goodyear engineer measures the temperature of a development tire after motorcycle racer Dale Singleton lapped the Daytona course during tire testing in 1981.

"We were getting more and more involved in Formula I, so we decided that these tires Kenny had designed could well be the start of something big. The only thing was, we were going to be making thousands of them, so we had to have a moldable design. We decided that if we made a pattern so complicated that the other guys couldn't carve it out on their tires, nobody could copy it."

Goodyear was on top in bike racing when they decided to bail out. The company had stopped making street motorcycle tires, and they figured it was pointless to make bike racing tires. It didn't prove anything to excel in a segment of the sport that would not result in the sale of more street tires.

After Goodyear pulled out, Carlisle tried to make dirt racing tires, but they didn't work too well. In fact, after one season the American Motorcycle Association called Goodyear and said, "You guys have to help us." As it turned out, if they had a one-hundred-lap race, they had to turn it into two fifty-lappers because the tires wouldn't last, so Goodyear came back and made dirt tires, just as a service to the sport. But they weren't called "motorcycle" tires—they were referred to as "dirt" tires.

Motorcycle racing was more than merely a memory, because the design Kenny Roberts had penciled out on a bike tread was, in fact, the origin of the Gatorback, which was later to become the world's most successful automobile rain tire.

The first automobile race in which the new rain tires were used was at Zolder in the Belgian Grand Prix. There was a saying that "It always rains in Belgium," so the Goodyear engineers decided to take along a goodly supply of the new rain tire.

"Michelin had this mystique that in rain they were always faster than Goodyear," Miller says with a hint of a smile. "Jody Scheckter, the reigning world champion, didn't even qualify for the race. I mean we smoked them. As he was walking back to the garage area, he said, 'I knew I was in trouble when Goodyear cars were passing me on both sides.' "

Didier Pironi in a Ligier won the race on Goodyears. The new rain tire had worked so well in practice that there was no question it was to be the standard for wet tracks. Few people knew that its origins went back to a motorcycle race.

Expansion Keeps Engineers Busy

Returning to four-wheeled vehicles, the battle was heating up on all fronts. "Trans-Am is probably the most exciting series I ever got involved in," says Mike Babich. It drew some big names from both the United States and Europe. For one thing, you had Ford and Chevy from the beginning—later American Motors' Javelin, Dodge's Challenger and the Plymouth 'Cuda were on the entry lists; Mark Donohue was in Roger Penske's Camaro for a couple of years and then in Penske Javelins, Parnelli Jones was in a Cougar at first and then Mustangs for the Bud Moore team, and Sam Posey ran the AutoDynamics Challenger. That alone would be enough for a great race.

Mark Donohue, above, drove in Trans-Am, Can-Am, Indy and endurance races during the '60s and early '70s.

Donohue, right, roared to another victory in his Javelin at the 1970 St. Jovite Trans-Am.

"But there were other guys, too. If you talked with Fran Hernandez, who ran Ford's program, he would tell you that Jerry Titus stood head and shoulders above the others. I heard Fran in the pit area one day in a heated discussion with mechanics over a change in a chassis set-up. He said 'You guys forget that you're comparing everybody to Jerry Titus; well, just forget it because he's worth half a second. Remember that.'

"Titus had the shortest career of almost any professional I know; any *good* professional, at least. He started late in life but he could tell you about a tire. He was very gentle on a car. I remember Jerry in a Shelby Mustang at Modesto, California," Babich recalls. "Everybody was grinding off tires on that old Navy strip like it was paved with sandpaper; but not Jerry. He was getting half again the tire wear as the rest.

"There also was George Follmer, who usually ran Goodyear; unless, of course, Firestone was faster and then he ran their tires. Most of the drivers ran whatever would get the job done. Eventually that's what brought everybody to us, including Peter Revson and Peter Gregg. It was a great series for Goodyear.

"For one thing," Babich points out, "the fact that our engineering department didn't run the show as they did across town, made a difference. Oh, there's nothing wrong with the engineers running things but there's always a tendency to try to protect yourself. When marketing runs it, as they did at Goodyear, all the cards are on the table—the deficiencies and all. That way you get them ironed out."

At Goodyear, the marketing department had the final say on what was going to be done. Racing was a sales tool.

"We had problems at Michigan one year and it was the marketing guys who decided to stop everything until they got the tire problems worked out. It wasn't up to the engineers to bite the bullet, and they were glad."

The SCCA Trans-American Series was a first class effort. Bob Tullius won the inaugural event in a Goodyear-equipped Dodge Dart. The race was held at the tough Sebring course March 25, 1966, within a separate

Sam Posey, bottom, was another multi-talented driver of the period; today as a TV broadcaster he shares his intimate knowledge of the racing scene with his viewers.

class run as part of the annual 12 Hours. This allowed Tullius to compete for a Trans-Am win as well as for overall position. It whetted the company's appetite for more, which wasn't long in coming—but if anything it heightened the tire war with Firestone, who also had some top drivers on their tires.

Trans-Am cars were far from showroom, although they looked something like it. There was a lot of fiberglass and a lot of horsepower—and with the top drivers the series attracted, it became a real crowd-pleaser. At one point the series pitted world-class drivers from Formula I, Indy and the sports car world against one another. It was exciting, but it died down when the factories pulled out. For one thing, the money wasn't there and, for another, neither was the spirit. The very same thing that had made NASCAR so popular—the competition among Ford, Chevy and Chrysler—was gone.

Pre-race lap prior to start of a Can-Am race at LaGuna Seca, California.The UOP Shadow, 101, was the only all-American car entered. Car 20 is a Porsche piloted by Jo Siffert of Switzerland, while No. 38 is a BRM with Britain's Brian Redman at the wheel.

A second major SCCA series, the Canadian-American Challenge, also started in 1966, an outgrowth of the United States Road Racing Championship. Sanctioned jointly by the Canadian Sports Car Club (CASC), there were two Canadian and no more than eight U.S. events annually. Can-Am was the opposite of Trans-Am—the cars were built from-the-ground-up race cars; no comparison whatsoever with your street car. These fast, non-production and possibly noisiest race cars drew top drivers from around the world. Bruce McLaren won the first of eighteen consecutive Can-Am races on Goodyears. The pace was picking up every day on East Market Street.

When it came to drivers, Can-Am drew the cream-of-the-crop, with men such as Jackie Stewart, John Surtees, Denny Hulme, McLaren, Brian Redman and David Hobbs rounding out the European contingent. They locked horns with Jim Hall and Hap Sharp in their Chaparrals, along with Peter Revson, Mark Donohue, Lothar Motschenbacher, George Follmer and Chuck Parsons—to name a few.

"The McLarens were popular and fast," recalls Lee Gaug, who later became manager of international racing for Goodyear. "The Porsches and the Penske cars also were highly competitive. It was like a condensed version of Formula I racing. At the end of the year the top guys would sell that year's cars to young drivers on their way up. It was unbelievable how much good equipment there was in that series."

Parnelli Jones, perhaps best known as an Indy driver, was a top contender in the Trans-Am series during the late '60s and early '70s.

Among the Trans-Am and Can-Am drivers of the late Sixties and early Seventies were, l to r, George Follmer, Peter Revson, and Bob Tullius.

Goodyear ran Sports Car Specials in the first Trans-Am races, but when it came to the powerful Can-Am cars, the engineers went back to the drawing board. They needed wider tires.

"The tire we had supplied for the 917 Porsche was the biggest tire we had," says Gaug. "On a twenty-one inch rim, it was twenty-eight and a half-inches tall and had an eighteen-inch tread width. The tire worked so well that we still use the same size and shape in modified racing.

"The cars were developing more than one thousand horsepower from the big, stock-block engines, so we had to develop a racing tire for all of them. And we discovered one important thing: The best tread pattern was no pattern at all. Slicks."

With the success of the Can-Am and Trans-Am series, a third was established: the SCCA Grand Prix (Formula 5000). At Continental Divide Raceway in Colorado, Gus Hutchinson used Goodyears to win the first-ever SCCA Grand Prix race on May 14, 1967, and went on to win the inaugural season championship.

Also using Goodyears, Dave Heinz drove his Corvette to an overall victory at Virginia International Raceway in the initial International Motor Sports Association (IMSA) GT race in 1971. Heinz and Bob Johnson drove another Corvette to a class victory in the 1972 six-hour Daytona Continental, which was eventually to become the Rolex 24, one of the two remaining major endurance races in the world, the other being the 24 Hours of LeMans.

Breaking into a new form of racing is more than an esoteric

Three more popular drivers of the period, l to r, Jackie Stewart of Scotland, Bob Bondurant, and Jo Siffert.

engineering exercise for Goodyear. The new product must have market value and, more often than not, must have the development support of a top racing team: A.J. Foyt and the Indy 500 tire; Dan Gurney and Jack Brabham in Formula I; Bob Glidden and the Pro Stock tire. Such was the case with two-time World of Outlaws sprint car champion Sammy Swindell and the Dirt Track Special.

"We took the drag tire and developed from there," says Swindell. "We got going in the right direction with the size and the profile and some of the compounds. Then Goodyear made a mold. We had to hand groove them but we got that right for the dirt tracks. We kept getting closer and closer, until we had the tire that worked perfectly."

It must have been close to perfect, anyway; Swindell convincingly won the World of Outlaws championship two years in a row on the new Goodyear tires.

With the millions of dollars both Goodyear and Firestone had spent

Lee Gaug led Goodyear's European racing operation from Akron and later concentrated on Formula I activities.

Denny Hulme at speed in the familiar No. 5 McLaren at a Can-Am series event.

Hulme waves checkered flag after winning Can-Am event.

Big News at Daytona... GOODYEAR RADIAL TIRES WIN FIRST TIME OUT!

Dave Heinz and Bob Johnson pilot Corvette No. 57 to a smashing victory in the over 2.5 litre Group IV GT Class.

In a gruelling contest that saw radials out front at the 6 hour Daytona Continental, Goodyear's new racing radial tires took the flag in the over 2.5 litre Group IV GT Class. Driving a punishing 163 laps, the Corvette completed 621.03 miles in 6 hrs. 1 min.—averaging 103.21 mph.

The Goodyear tires were the only radials to finish the race—and the first time radials had ever been on a winning car in a major class. This was a satisfying victory for Goodyear, a victory that brought to an end the notion that the making of radial tires is exclusive to foreign manufacturers.

Actually, Goodyear has had 13 years of experience in building radial tires. This experience counted heavily in developing the Blue Streak Sports Car Special radials that carried Heinz and Johnson to victory at Daytona.

Every Goodyear tire is made for a specific purpose. Goodyear tire engineers believe that a tire designed for the speed and torture of a racing track is totally unsuited for the road. And a road tire, designed for legal highway driving, would not, and could not, perform successfully on the track.

It is this principle of specific design that accounts primarily for the fact that, on both the track and the road, winners go Goodyear.

Dave Heinz, above. The Heinz and Bob Johnson car that won on Goodyear radials at Daytona is shown at right taking a turn at Sebring.

in developing the "perfect" tread design, they discovered that *no design* was the answer. Slicks gave them maximum traction.

"The tread design, to a certain extent, was a p.r. sales tool," muses Gaug. "It looked pretty, but it didn't make the tire work any better."

Mike Babich concurs with Gaug: "In the early compounds, the tread design helped a little in cooling the tire, but in some cases it worked just the opposite. The flexing of the tread caused the tire to build up more heat."

Suddenly, the one thing that both major tire companies had boasted about—the "ultimate tread design"—was a thing of the past. Scores of photos and news releases over the years had been to no avail.

The entire Can-Am series was getting a lot of attention. When the Porsche 917 came along, it was a giant killer. That brought even more interest. But it also was probably one of the downfalls of Can-Am. Because it was almost impossible for the other cars to compete against the powerful McLarens and the Porsches, it became increasingly difficult for the drivers to get much money from car builders to combat such formidable competition.

In spite of the success with slicks, tread design was not relegated to the trash bin. There was the matter of rain. European racing as well as American sports car racing was run, rain or shine. Slicks obviously were not going to work, so the efforts of Goodyear's earlier grooving and the subsequent molded rain tire became even more important.

"You have to displace the water," Gaug points out, "but once you've moved it, you have to have a compound that will adhere to the surface you're running on. Some compounds only work in hot weather and some in cold, but we found out that the best in rain is the cold weather one because it creates its own heat.

"The whole thing gave us the idea of further testing for a quad tire design. We went to our test track in Luxembourg. First we ran the tires on a glass plate, which enabled us to observe the tread action from underneath. We recorded the displacement pattern on the front tires, which were about ten and one-half inches wide, shooting for a design that would evacuate enough water so that the rear tires, when running over it, were tracking on a semi-dry surface—an area that already had a lot of the water thrown out of it.

"It's difficult to test a rain tire," Gaug emphasizes, "because the water is never the same. The line gets drier, the rain increases or slows down and certain places on the track are different than others because they drain off better or hold water. It's an ever-changing situation."

Performance at St. Jovite

It was to be the third consecutive Trans-Am win for American Motors. The weekend was hot, humid, and wet. Mark Donohue was Roger Penske's driver that year, campaigning an AMC Javelin.

Race day was August 2, 1970. The site: Mt. Tremblant track, St. Jovite, Quebec, Canada. A wet weekend—a number of delays in the schedule—and the delays usually occurred when the sun was shining!

Following the previous race, Mark Donohue and the Penske/Sunoco crew had planned their strategy: at Mt. Tremblant they would pit early at lap 14 and take on fuel, looking to gain an advantage when the

Continued on page 131

Fire was one of the major concerns of racing in the early days, before Goodyear developed the fuel cell and thereby reduced the risk of fire. It was one of two major safety contributions by the company, the other being the inner tire.

The whole maneuver was a perfect example of the tremendous amount of energy Goodyear was putting into racing.

On the home front, the company began further improvement on its fuel cell, which had been developed a decade before in 1955 by Goodyear and mandated by USAC after the terrible, fiery crash in the 1964 Indy 500. USAC said they had to be proven "crashworthy." Goodyear, not knowing exactly what it was they wanted, because the fuel cells they had developed had worked well in prior USAC races, responded with a design that met and exceeded Vietnam-era military

Race driver Chip Ganassi of Pittsburgh, Pennsylvania, compares a modern crashworthy Indy-car fuel cell developed by Goodyear with fragile drums strapped to the rear of 1912 and 1914 Indianapolis 500 cars.

helicopter fuel cell specifications and test requirements. It was a project in which they believed.

The Goodyear-developed fuel cells became one of the two most significant safety devices in racing. The other was the inner tire. There was no question among racing officials who had the best track record for

Continued from page 129

competition made their pit stops.

Mark's challengers were George Follmer and Parnelli Jones, both driving Mustangs for the Bud Moore teams.

Follmer pitted on lap 24 for tires and gasoline; Parnelli Jones was 15 seconds ahead of Donohue. The leaders were running Mustang, Javelin, Mustang.

On lap 28 Parnelli pitted but lost valuable time when he got sideways in pit lane because of intermittent rain and the water used to wash off the cars after refueling was making puddles of water and gasoline for a very slick road surface. This put Parnelli 29 seconds behind Donohue. Parnelli later went off the track into the "boonies" and was out of the race,

Continued on page 133

Bill Ludwick, Goodyear's chief fuel cell engineer, is shown putting the new fuel cells through one of the more basic tests.

safety. The drivers were even more aware.

Before the advent of the cells, there were many die-hard race fans who had trouble watching the start of a race. More accidents happened during the first few laps before the cars began to spread out than at any other time during the race. Several drivers had been killed; some of them had died because of fire. This no longer was as serious a threat.

There had been a period, in fact, when racing had turned sour to many because of the deaths. In NASCAR, Joe Weatherly, Tiny Lund, Fireball Roberts, Jimmy Pardue, and Billy Wade had died in crashes; USAC had lost Eddie Sachs, Davey MacDonald and Bobby Marshman.

"In Formula I, it was unbelievable," recalls Leo Mehl. "Here's what had happened in one year alone: On April 7th [1968] Jimmy Clark was killed, on May 7th Mike Spence died at Indy in a Lotus, on June 7th it was Ludovico Scarfiotti and on July 7th Jo Schlesser died in the French Grand Prix. When August 7th came, nobody wanted to get in a race car. But they did and nothing happened. Exactly one month later, Lance Reventlow died in a plane crash. Before I left Europe, Jo Siffert, Francois Cevert, Jochen Rindt, Pedro Rodriguez and Bruce McLaren were all killed."

In almost every crash there had been a fire. Goodyear and Firestone engineers were allowed to cross the pit walls to check tires, but when one

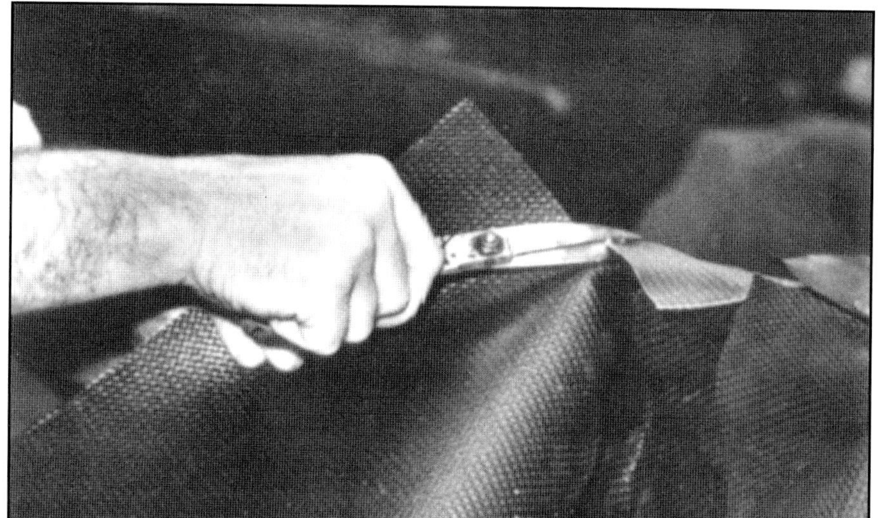

Fitting the outer skin to the fuel cell.

More of the testing procedures.

Goodyear developed and built the first fuel cells for race cars, greatly reducing the dangers of fire in race crashes. Every detail of production was carried out with precision.

Continued from page 131

leaving Follmer and Donohue in contention for the lead.

On lap 42 Penske pulled Donohue in for fuel, but no tire change—every second counted and Penske had decided, "Sometimes you have to roll the dice." Donohue was out again in 18 seconds; he was now 10 seconds behind Follmer and gaining one second per lap.

Follmer had to pit again on lap 47 for tires and to have a front fender fixed from contact with another car.

With Follmer making an extra tire change during that pit stop, Donohue was able to accumulate nearly a minute's lead. It was then

Continued on page 134

Crashworthy fuel systems built by Goodyear have all but eliminated fire as a hazard from the Indianapolis 500 race. Here engineer Ludwick is shown with wedge shape cells designed for the new "ground effects" cars for 1980.

of the Firestone engineers was badly hurt in a pit crash at Langhorne, Pennsylvania, the two companies got together and insisted that USAC prohibit anybody but actual pit crews from crossing the wall.

"All of us were apprehensive, to say the least. That's why we worked so hard at trying to make racing safer."

Competition Withdraws

The Indianapolis 500 in 1975 lacked one element that had been there since the first race in 1911—Firestone. In a move that stunned the entire racing world, Firestone announced at the end of the 1974 season that they were giving up USAC, NASCAR and Formula I automobile racing. Just like that!

The tire war had ended. In ten years from the time Goodyear showed up with their hats in their hands at Indianapolis, Firestone was gone. Goodyear had totally driven them from racing.

"It surprised everybody," says Mehl. "Particularly the drivers. A lot of them had been extremely loyal to Firestone and I guess they thought they would be looked on as second class citizens in the Goodyear camp.

Mario Andretti was a perfect example: He had been one of their chief testers and had driven practically every race on their tires since he started. He was amazed at the service he got with us. He couldn't believe we were giving him the same tires as we gave Foyt. It was a democracy he hadn't known. And, you know, he became one of our biggest friends, just because he was treated like everyone else.

"Al Unser, Sr., was the same way. Now anything you ask either of them to do, they'll bend over backwards."

"It wasn't so much that we simply outspent them—I guess we did—but we spent it wisely," Babich says with pride.

In early tests, we paid the drivers and car owners and agreed to rebuild any blown engines. Well, some of these guys would come in and run ten laps and change engines and then blow one and change again.

"We realized that we were paying for them to experiment on motors," he says. "We said, 'to hell with this,' and hired Herb Porter to build and maintain five engines. When we had a test, one of his motors went in the car. It saved us a lot of money, and we got better tests because we had uniform engines. We did this for about eight years, while Firestone was spending much more money on their tests by doing it the old way."

The joy that one might have expected from the Goodyear camp was somewhat tempered by the fact that even though they now had it all to themselves, it wasn't as much fun without competition.

The tire war, particularly at Indy, had ended on a bizarre note. The final result of the ten years of competition: Goodyear 95, Firestone 95.

Even though what Goodyear had done was an incredible accomplishment, the ninety-sixth win would be somewhat hollow without the guys in red to challenge them.

Still, it had been quite a feat. Everybody knew it.

Continued from page 133

Penske decided to call Donohue in. Donohue pitted for a change of tires on the right side only and was out. Five laps later Donohue took the checkered flag, 61.5 seconds ahead of Follmer. Only two tires were changed for the 70-lap race, and then only to maximize handling on a wet track.

Walt Czarnecki

(Walter Czarnecki was Performance Activities Manager for American Motors Corporation during this period; he is now Executive Vice President of Penske Corporation.)

"Big Daddy," the "Snake" and the "Mongoose" propel Goodyear to the top in Seventies drag racing battles.

The reputation Goodyear had established for fairness and honesty had spread worldwide, first in NASCAR and then at Indy and finally throughout Europe. They practiced exactly the same doctrine: Treat everybody the same.

"In Europe, Pirelli had given better tires to their favorite drivers; so had Michelin," says Stu Grant, manager of passenger tire programs. "Our policy was put into practice and everybody knew they could believe us. That's what keeps you in for the long haul; you have to operate in an honorable fashion.

"Take a guy like Frank Williams, a Formula I car-builder," Grant points out. "Because of the way we treated everybody, he has become one of our strongest supporters over the years. He would stick with us through thick and thin. But it wasn't easy because when we broke into Formula I racing we had many decades of tradition to overcome. Testing alone was very difficult; I mean, these cars had so much horsepower and were so light that it wasn't just as simple as taking some Indy tires over there and running them.

"We took three compounds for the first test and decided which worked best, so that's what we offered to everybody. I guess one of the reasons we were successful—beyond our integrity—was the fact that we had a wider range of stuff than the other guys. We bracketed weather conditions and took everything into consideration."

As tough as it had been to break into Indy and Formula I, drag racing was even more difficult. For one thing, it all had started in California in a very informal way; a bunch of guys took their street rods and streamliners to dry lake beds on weekends and raced against a clock. It instantly became the craze of the West Coast and spread rapidly throughout the entire nation.

At first, regular street tires were used but as the speeds grew, and as the sport expanded, the need for better compounds and wider tires became apparent. The hot set-up became recapping soft compound treads onto whatever racing casing they could find. Three Southern California recappers, Kasler, Bruce and Inglewood, led the way with the makeshift drag tires.

The first real drag tire was built by M&H in Watertown, Massachusetts. Marvin Rifchin formed a small company to build drag racing tires and the entire drag world flocked to his trucks at every meet. The tires were far from what are offered for today's 300-mile-per-hour quarter-mile speeds, but it beat anything that had been offered before. By a wide margin.

When Goodyear decided that they would be missing a broad segment of the racing world if they bypassed the drag strips, they began by recapping M&H tires with their own compounds for test purposes. It obviously was a stop-gap measure, but it at least got them to the drags and caused a few people to take note of the Wingfoot.

The first major Goodyear National Hot Rod Association (NHRA) victory was scored by Maynard Rupp in his Top Fuel dragster at the

Springnationals in Bristol, Tennessee. It was followed a couple of years later by Dick Landy in Pro Stock at the Summernationals in York, Pennsylvania. Victories were few and far between at first, so it became evident that they needed a new drag tire.

By the time Goodyear had developed its own real drag tire, Rifchin had taken another positive step in an effort to outperform his competition: He produced a tire that the drag crowd called the "wrinkle wall."

"Racers kept running their tires at inflation pressures considerably lower than the manufacturers were recommending," Rifchin recalls. "We had a six-ply sidewall tire that we recommended be raced at twenty-four pounds per square inch. Well, we discovered that most of these guys were running them as low as eight pounds per square inch, so we went to a four-ply sidewall. The sidewalls were so thin that they wrinkled, but the tires worked."

There was a major safety problem because the low inflation allowed the tires to slip on the rims and damage the tubes and valve stems.

In 1974 at Englishtown, New Jersey, M&H wrinkle-wall tires featured a heavily inflated safety shield inner liner—the liner Goodyear had developed a decade earlier for the entire racing world as a major safety factor. This inner liner clamped the bead to the rim.

The new M&H tire literally killed the recapping business. And it sent Goodyear back to develop its own wrinkle-wall tire.

"M&H was the big player of the day," says John Slikkerveer, who was Goodyear's drag racing field manager for a number of years. "It took us a long time to come into our own light, and if it hadn't been for 'Big Daddy' Don Garlits and his Top Fueler, we might not have been noticed even then. Garlits was the first of the big names to try our tires, and he has stuck with us for thirty years. Connie Kalitta was the next big name to mount Goodyears to his massive drive wheels."

The battle was on once more. Tires kept getting taller and wider; compounds got softer and the sidewalls wrinkled more. Finally NHRA placed a restriction on the escalation of tire sizes. They settled on thirty-six inches in diameter and seventeen inches in tread width for the big cars. At the time, Goodyear had a 37.5 X 18 on the drawing board.

"It's probably a good thing NHRA put a stop to the whole thing," says Slikkerveer. "It's hard to tell how big we would have had to go to keep up. I can tell you, we were prepared to take it to a much higher level. As it was, we stabilized on that size and have spent the last ten

Race tire engineer Vito Caravito weighs a Blue Streak Dragway stock tire in 1965. These tires weighed 20% less than other types, thus reducing unsprung vehicle weight and helping to shrink elapsed time records for the quarter-mile sprint. (Opposite page, top)

Wrinkle wall drag tire, 1969. (Opposite page, center)

Note thickness of cut section of drag tire being held by Goodyear engineer. Unlike much thicker auto tire sidewalls, the .08-inch-thick sidewalls of a 1981 Goodyear Eagle drag racing tire wind up under acceleration like a spring to help launch a 2,000-hp dragster from 0 to 250 mph in less than six seconds. (Opposite page, bottom)

years fine-tuning the tire. We have worked at making it more consistent and more reliable and in improving the uniformity of tires. Instead of size, we took it to a higher level of quality.

"We have probably put more effort into Pro Stock than anything else," Slikkerveer points out. "For one thing, Top Fuel is very hard to test. I'm not saying that we've turned our backs on the other classes, we haven't; it's just that Pro Stock has proven to be more beneficial. There are more Pro Stock cars now than there used to be. With Top Fuel cars it's just the opposite; where there were probably one hundred Top Fuel cars ten years ago, today there are only twenty-five or thirty. There used to be thirty-two dragsters at a meet, now you can barely get sixteen.

"The sportsman market has had a much larger expansion because it includes Super Stock and Stock Eliminator."

Bob Shaffer, who took over the reins in drag racing in 1975 and returned as its field manager in 1992, agrees with Slikkerveer: "If you wanted to sell tires, you had to be competitive in Pro Stock because it fed down through the ranks; it made the guys in Super Stock and the Gas classes aware of our product. They figured that if the Goodyears worked on Pro Stock, then they had to work on their cars."

The one thing that probably helped Goodyear's drag racing program as much as anything else was when Bob Glidden chose them in 1976. Glidden, who has won nine World Championship crowns and eighty races, became readily acknowledged as one of the world's pre-eminent drag racers. He took Goodyear with him to the top.

"We went to Bob and asked if he would be interested in helping us develop a tire for Pro Stock racing," says Shaffer. "He agreed and we did a lot of testing, trying out all sorts of tires. We went strictly on how he felt about each tire. We used the new tires a few times in 1976, but it was the following year before we started running them on a consistent basis."

"We spent a lot of hours at the track," recalls Glidden, "testing from early morning to late in the day and slowly but surely, the Goodyear tire became better and better. I'd say that in a two-and-one-half-year period, Goodyear built something that was superior to anything available in Pro Stock racing."

Basically it's where the Pro Stock tire has been ever since.

"Raymond Beadle in the *Blue Max* Funny Car was another big step for Goodyear. Beadle came up from Texas and started using Goodyears. It sure helped us sell drag racing performance," recalls Shaffer.

It wasn't until Beadle beat Don "The Snake" Prudhomme that Funny Car drivers began to take Goodyear seriously. Even Prudhomme. In typical racer fashion, he decided, "If you can't beat 'em, join 'em." He, too, switched to Goodyear.

Once Prudhomme, who had the dominant Funny Car, switched, so did Don "The Mongoose" McEwen. It was an all-out war between "The Snake" and "The Mongoose." If one didn't pay strict attention, he might think the commentators were announcing a wrestling match. When Prudhomme became the first man in drag racing to turn in a five-second run at Ontario, California, in 1976, Goodyear drag tires were propelled to the top of the heap. Garlits surely had started it all. Glidden and Prudhomme and Kalitta picked up the ball and ran for the goal line time after time. In fact, it was Garlits's car that broke the 250-mile-per-hour barrier. Garlits wasn't driving because he was feuding with NHRA at the time, so he turned the reins over to Jerry Ruth, who piloted the car to a mark at which everybody had been shooting for years. He did it on Goodyears at Englishtown.

From Track to Highway

"We rose to the challenge. We became the experts," says Bob Toth, marketing manager of high performance tire sales. "We took what we had and said 'this is an opportunity to apply racing tire technology to street tires,' and we did it at the worst possible time, right after the gas crunch of the early Seventies. While we were talking about mega horsepower, low quarter-mile times and high acceleration, without worrying about *stopping* the car or even *turning* it, everybody was

The monster truck, Crusher, *lives up to its name.*

Caught in mid-air, Bandit *is about to further reduce the height of the cars below.*

running around the streets in econoboxes.

"We were working on flat, superwide tires; the country was looking for anything to make driving more interesting in their little street machines, so we refocused from the maximum quarter-mile time and looked at what else we could do to appeal to the average motorist. We said, 'Okay, it takes a while to get up to sixty, so what can we do to make a tire that will maintain sixty right through this turn?'

"It's where the tires could really shine," recalls Toth. "They became more important than anything else on the car and the focus moved to not only power but to sophisticated chassis and tire designs. The chassis design engineer's sole purpose was to produce better handling through subtle refinements. How to better plant the tire was the key. But the tire could easily limit his ability to accomplish his job. That's where our racing experience came in. Roger Penske's newest chassis still would be going eighty if he was using 1951 Studebaker tires—I don't care what kind of money he spent in the wind tunnel."

It was precisely this kind of logic that caused Goodyear to begin shifting more and more technology from the race track to the highway.

Radial Race Tires

What was left? Goodyear was in command in the red hot NASCAR Winston Cup series; Championship Auto Racing Teams (CART) had taken over the Indy car series and the Wingfoot clan was all alone there; they had taken control of Formula I racing and were now the major power in drag racing.

In less than two decades, Goodyear had become the dominant force in world racing. But there were changes brewing.

Now they looked beyond the asphalt lanes and into the dirt. Off-Road. Why not? It was about the only mountain left for them to conquer. It was a big one, but they were used to climbing.

Bill Hopkins, general manager of M.P.V. and specialty tires, was asked to start a design group for truck tires. "We needed to start focusing on light truck tires because we were losing our market share there," Hopkins recalls.

He accepted the challenge, and development and testing began. "One thing became quite evident," says Hopkins, "you can't b.s. truck customers. You have to go to them with something substantive, so we knew we had to have the right product, otherwise we would be out in the cold.

"We started off by using street tires, but competition was getting tougher, so I decided to go after them. The top trucks were using thirty-

Goodyear developed unique off-road racing tires for the Hurst-sponsored "Baja Boot" race cars. In its first outing on the fat Goodyear Baja Special tires in 1968, the "Baja Boot" won its class in a race at Riverside, California. With the car is Ed Pearlman, president of the National Off Road Racing Association.

three-inch-tall tires, so we built a thirty-five-incher. There had been an inordinate amount of flat tires in off-road racing. We discovered that it was mostly due to broken wheels; the trucks were bottoming, so when we increased the diameter of the tire and developed different constructions, it helped tremendously.

"We took a lot of racing technology and started to look at it; in fact, that's how the Wrangler GSA came about."

As they had done in most other forms of racing, Goodyear hired the tops in the field to do the initial testing; in off-road racing it was Walker Evans. At first Evans balked. "I'm not putting those big tires on my truck," he told Goodyear, but Hopkins countered with, "Wait a minute, all we want you to do is evaluate them. We think we've got something that will work."

Evans tried the tires. Much to his amazement, they did work. He confessed later, "I guess I gave you guys a hard time, but I'm really glad you kept after me. The new tires work." He has been a staunch Goodyear supporter ever since.

"Walker found some benefits that the engineers hadn't even discovered. We helped him with his suspension and he certainly helped us with our new tire," related Hopkins.

Test tires for what became the Wrangler Radial tire are on the off-road race vehicle of champion driver Walker Evans (right). Evans worked closely with Goodyear engineers in designing the Wrangler Radial.

There was a high degree of confidentiality between Goodyear and the teams with which they worked—regardless of whether they were off-road, motorcycle, Formula I, sports cars, Indy or NASCAR. To be able to really help the teams, they had to know what the teams were doing, suspension-wise and even engine-wise. The teams had to confide a lot of their secrets to the Goodyear engineers if they were going to get any significant help tire-wise.

Goodyear kept this information to themselves because they couldn't afford to lose the faith of even one team. It was part of their overall program of confidence building. This became very important because the company had one of the biggest tricks up its sleeve that they had ever had. Goodyear had a new tire, which they intended to move into many different racing arenas.

The new tire was a radial. It had been a long time coming. Michelin had experienced a great deal of success with radials, so Goodyear decided it was time to find out what this type of construction would do compared to the bias-ply tires they had been running since they got back into racing in the Fifties.

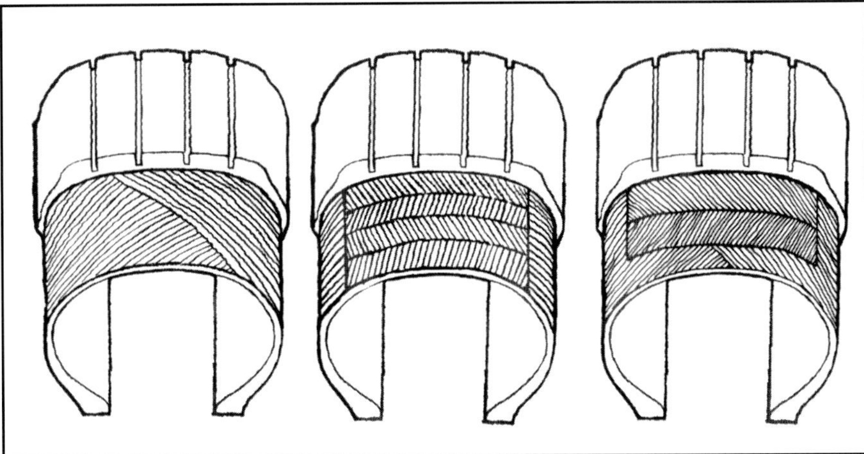

Note the differences among the three tires: bias-ply, radial-ply and bias-belted. In a conventional bias-ply tire (left) the cords cross the tire at an angle. In a radial-ply tire (center) the cords run straight across, and an additional layered belt of fabric is placed between the plies and the tread. The bias-belted tire (right) combines these concepts, with the cords crossing at an angle and a belt between the plies and tread.

As Hopkins's background had been in Europe working with speed rated tires, Tom Barrett, Goodyear's chairman, asked him to start a program which might convert all of their racing efforts from bias to radial tires. He was named manager of radial race tire engineering, under Vince Prus, Vice President of Technology, one of Goodyear's greatest racing division supporters.

The company's Formula I production facility at Wolverhampton had been closed and Formula I race tire manufacturing moved to Akron.

Former Chairman of the Board and CEO Charles Pilliod had said, "Since most of our highway-use tires are radial, we should race radial tires." When the boss speaks, you listen.

"With Michelin as our competition," says Hopkins, "we knew it wasn't going to be an easy task. Where should we start? Well, we figured the first thing we had to do was beat ourselves. In the Fall of 1982, our goal was to have a Formula I radial rain tire in time for the Monaco Grand Prix the following year.

"The rain tire was a perfect place to start, because one of the biggest advantages a radial tire has is that the tread stays open; you can evacuate the water out of it. But before we began testing, we had to first develop the whole product, from the lab to the test track."

Formula I driver Patrick Tambay tested early Goodyear radials.

With no fanfare at all, Patrick Tambay had raced on a set of extra-wide, experimental Goodyear radial tires in the 1978 British Grand Prix at Brands Hatch. He finished sixth. The tires were put on the shelf for four more years. Now it was time to pull them off the shelf and begin further development.

Goodyear asked its machine design people, headed by Jim Stokes, to take a clean sheet of paper and design a radial racing tire building machine; they didn't want a cobbled-up passenger or truck tire machine. They wanted something specifically designed to build racing tires.

The engineers talked about what was needed and what they wanted from a manufacturing standpoint. It had to be a first-rate, top-of-the-line manufacturing system that would give them uniformity and quality, race after race.

They had to reeducate the tire builders. No longer was one-quarter of an inch close enough; they started to talk in terms of millimeters. Before the machines might produce tires that were 25.5 inches in diameter on one set, 25.7 on the next and 26.1 on another. When they got to the radials, they were astounded; 25.96, 25.95, 25.96. Every tire was exactly the same. The days of working with the non-uniformity of tire diameter to get the car set up right were gone. Now the teams had to work on the chassis and springs and other suspension components.

Goodyear began tests on the new tire at Daytona on the road course in November 1982. They wet down the tightest part of the race course. The tires worked, so the next plateau was a test at Toronto, Canada where tests using a Ferrari were conducted with Michele Alboreto driving, who set a track record on the new tires.

"We were really beginning to get things dialed in," explained Hopkins. "But when we brought the radial to Formula I, we didn't make much fuss about it. We didn't want people talking about us, because usually when they talked about a product, it was negative. We wanted to be like a roll cage, not even mentioned. We wanted to be sort of a non-factor but, all of a sudden, good things were being said about us and we found that we liked it."

The one thing Goodyear and the drivers alike found was that the radials were extremely consistent. "It was unbelievable," says Hopkins. "Before a team like, say, Ferrari would send a semi-trailer load of tires to be measured and put off in sets of fifty-thousandths increments of stagger. With the radials there was almost no difference in the size of a truckload of tires.

When Michele Alboreto tested the new FI racing radial rain tires at Toronto, he set a new track record.

Goodyear's new racing radial rain tire for Formula I cars recorded fastest lap times during rainy practice sessions at both the Detroit and Monaco Grands Prix in 1983. The racing radial features the same unidirectional "gatorback" tread pattern used to improve wet traction of the Eagle VR50 street radial designed for the 1984 Chevrolet Corvette.

"We actually had to build a stagger tire because of the tremendous uniformity of the radials. They became a far more precise entity, and that was good because the last thing an engineer wants to hear is 'We got a bad set of tires.' "

When it came time to test, they went to tracks like Paul Ricard in southern France or Estoril in Portugal or Imola in Italy because it was reasonably warm all year. If Michelin was testing, they allowed Goodyear to come and test also. Goodyear did the same thing with them or with Pirelli. It wasn't like Indianapolis where there was so much secrecy. "If you ran a fast time, nobody knew if the tire would go five laps or one hundred," says Lee Gaug. It didn't show them anything, so there was no reason why we couldn't go testing at the same track with someone else. We did our thing, they did theirs.

"In the first tests we had three full contract teams—Ferrari, Williams and McLaren. For drivers we had only the finest—guys like Nelson Piquet, Alan Jones and Didier Pironi. Our philosophy always has been that you learn a lot more about the tires if you use the best equipment and the best drivers available. It's worked for us."

Alain Prost awaits adjustments to his McLaren at the Paul Ricard circuit in France in 1984, where Goodyear did a lot of its testing.

Race tire engineer Tim Miller calls up a computer image of the radical new (1980) Formula I rain tire tread design he created, nicknamed "gatorback."

It worked so well that the first Eagle Formula I radial was raced in March of 1984 at the Brazilian Grand Prix. Every Formula I race after that was run on radials.

Alboreto drove his Ferrari to victory in the Belgian Grand Prix at Zolder. It was the first of hundreds of wins for Goodyear Eagle radials in Formula I.

"What we were getting from racing from a technical standpoint was phenomenal," says Tim Miller, area account manager of tire applications. "It was invaluable in producing a high performance street tire, and even more so when we began working with radials. We were the proving ground for new carbon blacks and oils and polymers and we could concentrate on the material side of tire development.

"Working in racing was a great place because things happen so fast. In other areas of the company, there was a great lull between the idea and the final product. In racing, if a tire was made, it could be sold within a matter of weeks. Everything we did was immediately transferable to the automotive side of tire development.

"The material developments were wonderful," Miller continues. "The lessons we learned in racing taught us all responsibility and accountability; a race is going to happen on a particular date and you had to make decisions to be there with the right tire at the right time."

When Goodyear showed up at their first Formula I race, the tires were white lettered. It was the first time anybody in Europe had seen that. The closest thing any of them had seen was a small "Dunlop" on some of the driver's uniforms. There were no decals on the cars. "After all," they said, "this is a gentleman's sport." Gentlemanly or not, the "Goodyear" white lettering stayed and, little by little, the cars began to appear with various corporate logos, until they began to resemble American racing cars.

Goodyear had opened the door to more sponsors and the sport benefited from it. Purses increased rapidly, as did world interest in the sport of Formula I.

Radial Conversion Continues

It was the Eighties—a time of experimentation. Tires worked better when they were warmer, everybody knew that, but the only way to get them warm was to put them on the race car and run it hard. This took time and during a race if a car went out of the pits with a new set of tires, it often took a couple of laps to get them hot enough to work right. Lotus had an answer: They introduced electric tire blankets in 1983 at

American Peter Revson in his Formula I McLaren in 1973.

Hockenheim, Netherlands, where team "tire roller" Clive Hicks literally burned up the first set of tires he tried to heat with the blankets, earning the appellation "Clive Hicks and his hot slicks."

The blankets wrapped around the tire like a heating pad. They fit tightly, so the drivers had four "hot" tires waiting in the pits for them. The crews finally figured out everything; tire heaters became the standard way to keep tires warm in Formula I racing. They also enabled the teams to control air pressure.

A tire obviously has more pressure when it is hot than when it's cold. Before the blankets, they had to guess at what the pressure would be when the tire heated up; they had to stay four or five pounds under the optimum "hot" pressure.

Formula I was a consummate place to begin the radial program. "We would never have been able to beat some of the teams without radials," says Stu Grant, now manager of passenger tire programs. "But when we became successful, Michelin, who had been on the verge of dropping out, made up their minds to call it quits. With the exception of a few cars running on Pirellis, we had it all.

"The cars continued to develop more horsepower and we continued to develop faster tires. The rules which had been rewritten in 1981 had given us virtually unlimited tire size, but when the speeds went up drastically, they changed the rules again, limiting the tire size to twenty-six inches in diameter by an eighteen-inch cross-section width. Actually it made the cars go faster because they had less area out there in the wind.

"We had reached the tire limit by that point and maybe Michelin could see it coming. Eventually Pirelli pulled out, so once again we had an entire series to ourselves.

"We think Michelin will be back one of these days because Formula I is so important in Europe," Grant says. "For them to completely walk away from racing has to hurt them because in Europe all they have is soccer and auto racing. It's not like the States where we have half a dozen major sports.

"In Formula I, it's the drivers who are recognized; the cars are second. The French, for example, are fiercely national so they miss not having a French tire company in racing. But I guess they just couldn't

Formula I driver Carlos Reutemann (left) discusses tire strategy with Goodyear engineer Kevin Brenneman. At the time this photo was taken, Reutemann was leading Piquet by a single point for the 1981 FI title.

keep up at that point. Again it was a tribute to the fortitude of our team. They started at the bottom and took over. It's a little like starting a basketball team and immediately taking on the Chicago Bulls. You get knocked down a lot but you get right back up. You learn something each time.

"We've managed to do this sort of thing time after time," Grant says proudly. "It's been possible because we've had top management support every step of the way. Even with the financial problems the company has had on and off, we have had very few budget cuts. There have been some who have said 'Let's get out of it,' but cooler heads prevailed in the end. We've had the patience and courage to weather out the bad times and enjoy the good ones.

"There have been many challenges, but with the broad base of experience we have, we have a lot of guns we can point at somebody," Grant emphasizes.

"The major reason that it didn't take long for Goodyear to be accepted in European racing was because, from the beginning, they practiced the same kind of spirit that they had in the United States, by being fair and honest with everybody. There was no favoritism to any team," Grant reiterates.

"In the early days we might take a couple different sizes and maybe four different compounds, but we gave the tire that worked best to everybody," Gaug echoes. "Some of the other companies found out at times that they didn't have enough of the best, so they gave them to their favorite drivers. That made everybody else angry with them.

"That's why we always made sure we had enough tires for everybody. We had the happiest teams in Formula I racing, particularly the former Michelin and Pirelli guys."

"The development of the superspeedway radial tire was our biggest technical challenge of the radial race tire development program," says Stu Grant. "We knew that from the beginning. Not only did the tire have to carry the loads on the high banks at the tremendous Indy-car speeds, but it also had to handle well and provide good driver feedback. We approached the whole project very cautiously, and slowly worked up to the challenge.

"First it was Formula I, then Indy-car road course tires, then IMSA road course tires, then Indy-car short track oval tires and finally it was the Indy car superspeedway program. So after three years of concentrated radial tire development, we were ready.

"We decided on Michigan [International Speedway] because it was higher banked than Indy and after verifying our durability at Michigan we would have time to fine tune the handling and go to Indianapolis next year—Indy being the real focus of the whole program. We probably ran half a million miles on the lab wheel exceeding the Michigan service conditions in order to satisfy the durability requirements. After that we had a number of track test sessions at Michigan to be sure our handling was acceptable. After all the preparation was done, we were ready and we were confident."

Preparation for the 1985 Michigan 500 began and everything went extremely well. No handling problems whatsoever and speeds were fast. Friday ended and things were quite normal. Qualifying ended Saturday and with about one hour to go in the last practice session before the race, Roberto Guerrero came by the Start/Finish line with a flat right front tire. Everyone in the pits could see the problem with his right front tire. They went right to Roberto to get his comment on what happened and to look at the tire. As they were in the process of doing this—they

Don "The Snake" Prudhomme pushes his Funny Car to its limit in 1977.

Shirley Muldowney, considered the greatest woman driver in history by many, races to victory at the peak of her career in 1977.

Electric tire warmers first came on the scene at Formula I events in the Eighties. Pictured here are the current yellow-lettered Eagles being warmed up.

One of the all-time sprint car greats, Sammy Swindell, in action in 1981.

Scott Douglas put the pedal to the metal in his Walker Evans Racing, Goodyear-shod, Jeep off-road truck.

Drag racing great Don "Big Daddy" Garlits awaits the green light in the 1977 Springnationals.

Cars, trucks, motorcycles—and plowing contests! Goodyear's competitive interests encompass a broad range of activities.

Here a competitor in the 35th Annual World Plowing Contest makes final adjustments to his Goodyear-tired tractor. The event was held at the World Agricultural Exposition in September, 1988, at Amana, Iowa.

Rob MacCachren jumps across a Wisconsin off-road course.

were actually talking to Roberto in the garage—they heard over the public-address system that Bobby Rahal had crashed in Turn Two.

What was apparent to everyone in the place was that within fifteen minutes two cars had right front problems and Bobby had crashed hard. Bobby wasn't able to tell them much and the right front tire was impossible to examine since that corner of the car had hit the wall. "We looked hard at what we had—two right front tire incidents in a very short time span," Grant recalls. "We tried to be as objective as possible, but since it was the debut of the superspeedway radial, there was a degree of apprehension from the outset, and the events of the last few minutes hadn't exactly eased everyone's minds. Punctures are not an unusual occurrence, especially at Michigan, but these tires were different so there was a degree of uncertainty.

"Ultimately it came down to this: If we could have said with certainty that the two tires were definitely cut and run flat, we could have continued. But we just weren't able to say that without a detailed analysis so we did the only correct thing possible to do at that point—postpone the race for a week. We met with all the drivers and chief mechanics at one point and their faith in us was truly amazing. They simply said if you say it's okay to race, we'll race—if not, we won't—no second thoughts, no hesitation. Goodyear, you make the call. Everyone involved did their job. Roger Penske and Dan Luginbuhl, Penske's p.r. chief, were terrific—professional and supportive. Mike Babich did a fantastic job as well.

"In spite of the frustration, anger, and embarrassment, we did the unthinkable and postponed the Michigan 500 and did out best to explain to the press and our management what we had done. The bias-tire race took place the next weekend and the next year we went to Pocono [Pennsylvania] for our superspeedway radial debut. With a repave at Michigan that year we ended up actually doing the Indy 500 before we went back to Michigan, but in the end we did Michigan on radials as well and the Indy-car radial conversion was complete.

"As bad as it was to postpone the race, the reaction in the press was all positive. We were praised for our wisdom, our courage, and our respect for the safety of the drivers. What we did was simply the right thing to do—it was the *only* thing to do," Grant says.

Goodyear had a reputation to uphold.

Auto racing is the showcase for the cutting edge of automotive technology

"When you look back at what we've accomplished in motorsports, I think one of our biggest strengths is that we are part of the fraternity; we're a mainstay, a long term player," says Bob Toth, marketing manager for high performance tires. "We got in long before the real magnitude of the sport became apparent to most other companies. And now we have dedicated our energies to maintaining our presence and continuity and making sure we fend off all competition."

When it was announced in 1977 that the 1979 Indianapolis 500 Pace Car would be a Ford Mustang, Goodyear was pleased. When they found that the Mustang would pace the race on Michelin TRX radials, the racing division went into orbit. "Naturally Mr. Pilliod was not enthralled with the fact that Michelin tires would lead the field of thirty-three Goodyear-equipped Indy race cars," says Toth, "so it turned into an emotional debate with Ford. They said the car had been specially tuned around the Michelins. And then they added, 'You guys don't have a tire that compares.'

"That was all it took. We didn't have the exact car so we didn't know what our tires would do, but we began the challenge; we were going to design a tire that would outperform the TRX. We spent the next year and one-half—summer at Indy and winter at Ontario [California]—running a Mustang we had built-up, lap after lap to find out how many laps before a right front tire would blister," recalls Toth.

"The Mustang Pace Car was originally supposed to be a four-cylinder turbo, but late in the program they dropped in a V-8. The engine was heavier and the car was pushing like crazy in the turns. After literally hundreds of construction iterations we had our tires working, so we said, 'Okay, it's time to compete.' We ran our evaluation program at Indy with Dan Gurney driving. They brought their car and their Michelin tires; we brought ours. After about six laps, their tires blistered.

"Our tires ran and ran and ran. Their engineers watched in amazement. 'Okay, you've got it. We don't want anything to happen in front of 400,000 people,' they said."

Goodyear engineer Bob Toth (above) compares the tread width of an Eagle NCT high-performance street radial with that of a 1960-style auto tire. Bob Tullius used the Eagle NCT at Sebring 1981. It is twice the width of the street tires on which Tullius first raced in 1961.

Race driver K. Dana Roehrig (right)and a tire engineer discuss the racing performance of Goodyear's ultra-high-performance street tire, the Wingfoot Radial, prior to the start of the 1979 12 Hours of Sebring. In background are stacks of Goodyear racing tires used by the other racers.

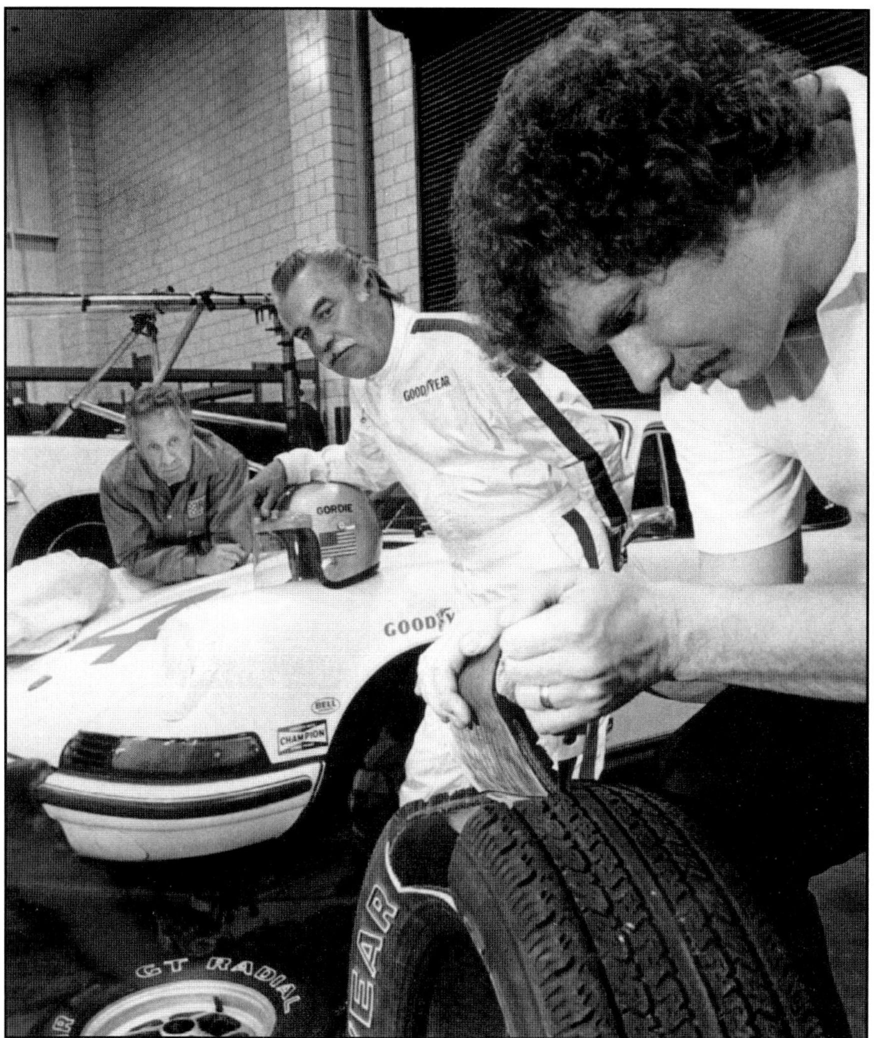

A Goodyear race tire engineer cuts a section of a Customgard GT Radial auto tire that was tested on the 3.82-mile road course at Daytona International Speedway. The high-performance street tire was introduced in the 1976 24 Hours of Daytona where it ran at speeds of up to 165 mph on a Porsche 911S. Behind the car is Lee Gaug.

The Wingfoot radial made its debut on the 1979 Indy Pace Car. Later in the year, Chevrolet came to Goodyear and expressed interest in the Wingfoot Radial. They wanted to evaluate the tire, and they did! They tested it against the Michelin, Pirelli P7s and Kleber.

"What came out of that program was a tire that looked very much like the Wingfoot," says Toth, "except that it was white-lettered and steel belted. The result was the Eagle GT. It became the first original equipment Eagle.

"Our performance tire line consisted of a Wingfoot, an Eagle and a Customgard radial. Nothing made sense. The Eagle was a steel-belted tire but it wasn't speed-rated; the Wingfoot was an aramid-belted fabric tire, and the superior performer of the three, and the Customgard was a full-belted aramid, but it had inferior compounding and wasn't much of a performer."

The marketing and sales group, headed up by Jim Barnett, laid out a strategy to tie the whole thing together. They approached Leo Mehl, who had been named director of Goodyear's entire racing program, and said, "We have a marketing concept that we would like to implement."

Mehl listened. "We'd like to create a conduit through which the consumer can better associate our motorsports activities with our street activities," they emphasized. "We need more than a high performance tire on the track, we need it on the street. We want a brand name. We want a high-performance product family."

Mike Babich, retired, was Assistant Director of Racing.

Barnett asked Mehl to come up with a common name. Mehl and Mike Babich agonized for hours, passing over "Eagle" at first because Goodyear was already using the name. Finally they settled on "Eagle," called Bob Gray in the advertising department and asked him to trick up a race tire with "Eagle" 180 degrees opposite "Goodyear" on the tire.

Former Grand Prix driver Dan Gurney (right) puts Eagle high-performance street tires to the wet braking test at Goodyear's San Angelo, Texas test track.

After he and Babich set the tire in a stand, Mehl showed it to Barnett, telling him, "We'll immediately set wheels in motion to restamp our molds if you agree with 'Eagle.' " Barnett agreed, and the "Eagle" family of performance tires was born, with the Eagle race tire the "Grand Daddy" of them all.

Goodyear first provided "Eagle" race tires at the 1980 Mosport Can-Am in Canada, and announced that "Eagle" would replace "Blue Streak" as the official designation for their racing tires. At the same time, a new high-performance street tire line also was dubbed "Eagle."

And this brought Goodyear's racing heritage right to the public. "There actually was a marketing plan to take motorsports and turn it into a value that could clearly be demonstrated through the name association

Leo Mehl, Director of Racing, left, with an elite group of Goodyear test drivers—(l. to r.) Dan Gurney, A.J. Foyt, and Richard Petty—at the San Angelo test track in 1981.

in the product line," explains Toth. "Not only could the consumer relate better, but so, too, could the auto manufacturer.

"It was a true measure of the performance advantage, but the differences are subtle. Our competitors are fairly good, and we are always struggling for that leading edge, but they are close behind us. The Eagle line gave us an advantage.

"If a manufacturer decides to take a base and turn one model into something sporty, they would start with—for example—pin stripes, maybe a hood scoop, some bucket seats, a leather-wrapped steering wheel and the gear-shift lever would go on the floor. That's a start. Those things give it pizzazz. To further position the car in the sport, especially the high-performance, market they would look to suppliers with the 'Right Stuff' and perhaps add gas-charged shocks and Goodyear Eagle performance tires.

"That image," Toth insists, "is so important that you as the consumer would feel like a 'wimp' to buy a base model on regular tires.

"The Chevrolet Lumina is used on the NASCAR Winston Cup circuit and customers relate to that. They forget that the car on the track is rear-wheel drive and the showroom car is front-wheel drive. That's irrelevant. And that's where you really begin to market *the image.*"

Motorsports is good not only for the company's image, but for its spirit. "I'm confident that our involvement in motorsports keeps us sharp. It teaches our engineers to think on their feet and ties us more closely with original equipment because, let's face it, the leading breakthroughs in automotive technology are debuted on the track.

"Today we have the leading performance street tire brand in history, and it's largely because of our racing success. Goodyear Eagle is on all

The racing debut of Goodyear's Eagle VR50 "Gatorback" street radial tire helped take a prototype Chevrolet Camaro Z28 to victory in the June 26, 1983 Longest Day of Nelson *at Nelson Ledges, Ohio. The Dick Guldstrand-prepared Z28 was driven on a shaved P245/50VR16 version of the tire by Jim Cook, Don Knowles and Bob Carradine at an average 80.3 mph, becoming the first American-made car to win the world's only 24-hour endurance race for showroom stock cars on street-legal tires.*

four corners of nearly every race car, but we're not a sponsor; we're a participant. A competitor," Toth exclaims. "And if we've done our racing job well, our passenger tires will sell well. It's that simple. Auto racing is the showcase for the cutting edge of automotive technology."

Engineering and Manufacturing Consolidate

The concept of a technical center where all Goodyear racing tires would be built was one that resulted from a meeting with city and county fathers trying to keep production facilities in Akron. By the Eighties all highway-use tire production in the city had been moved to various places throughout the nation. Akron had been dubbed "Rubber City" shortly after the turn of the Twentieth Century, but little by little the half-dozen rubber companies had decided that it was more practical to build their tires elsewhere.

Akron's air no longer smelled of rubber.

In a move designed to help the City of Akron, Goodyear made a decision to rebuild its aging Plant Two as a technical center for road and race tires and as a production facility for racing.

"We could no longer build racing tires on conventional tire machines," says Mehl. "Truck tire machines were too tall and passenger tire machines were not wide enough, so our new board chairman, Bob Mercer, asked Tom Barrett, then president, to design a new tire machine for us—and fast. Jim Stokes and his machine design group went to work.

"The precision required for a radial race tire had become much higher than for a passenger tire. At Indy, for instance, a size difference between the left side and right side tires (called stagger) of .05 of an inch would make a big difference in handling. That's about the thickness of a three by five index card folded over twice. But that would make the car so loose you couldn't even handle it. We needed a really special degree of accuracy," Mehl points out.

In 1983, Goodyear consolidated all of its race tire manufacturing and engineering facilities under one roof at its new $125 million World Technical Center. The move made possible the completion of the race tire "radialization" program. The remodeling of Plant Two had provided a futuristic Tech Center from the all but abandoned 73-year-old tire factory, turning it into an ultra-modern, high-tech operation. The entire race tire manufacturing operation was consolidated into a huge 700,000 square foot facility, where more than 600 technicians produced race tires and thousands of prototype and experimental highway use tires annually.

"One major goal in building the Goodyear Technical Center," says Fred Kovac, Vice President of Strategic Planning and Business, "was to create the ideal environment for the design and manufacture of racing tires for every application—that we are building now and others that we can only imagine."

Not Always a Smooth Ride

Goodyear was up to its corporate neck in motorsports, and every program was running smoothly. Most of the time.

"Our Formula I tires weren't right at Imola in 1986," recalls Lee Gaug. "In fact, we thought they might not be safe. We recalled them one day before the race and it turned out to be the best logistical exercise we ever had. We had some tires stored at Wolverhampton that had worked well in Brazil, so we began to make arrangements to get them to us [by air] in Italy.

"Brenda Vernor was the secretary to the president of Ferrari. She was British but she spoke Italian, so she was our liaison person. Tony Shakespeare and Barry Griffin were in charge of our Wolverhampton service crew. We all got together on the phone and figured out what we had in England and what we had to do to get them to Imola.

"It took seven or eight calls to find a charter plane big enough to haul a couple of hundred tires. Then we had to find pilots and a trucking company that could get the tires to the airport in England.

"We had the tires loaded up and trucked down to Stansford near Wembley, where the plane was. Everything was running smoothly until the truck was late in getting to Stansford. There was a noise abatement

Goodyear's Technical Center (left) in Akron, Ohio, which is not only headquarters for racing tire development and production, but the brain center for Goodyear worldwide.

Three views of tire production in process (center left, and two top photos on the opposite page).

Race tire builder Clyde George, bottom left, puts the finishing touches on a tire designed specifically for the September 25, 1983 Grand Prix at Brands Hatch, England. Each Goodyear Formula I racing tire is assembled from many components by a skilled craftsman at the Tech Center.

X-ray technician Dave Gordon, bottom right, examines a tire prior to shipment to Brands Hatch in 1983.

While Goodyear racing tires undergo numerous mechanical inspections including X-ray and holography, final inspection is still performed by skilled hands. In the bottom photo, opposite page, final inspector Lloyd Bowers (right) and Leo Mehl inspect Formula I tires destined for the 1983 Brands Hatch event.

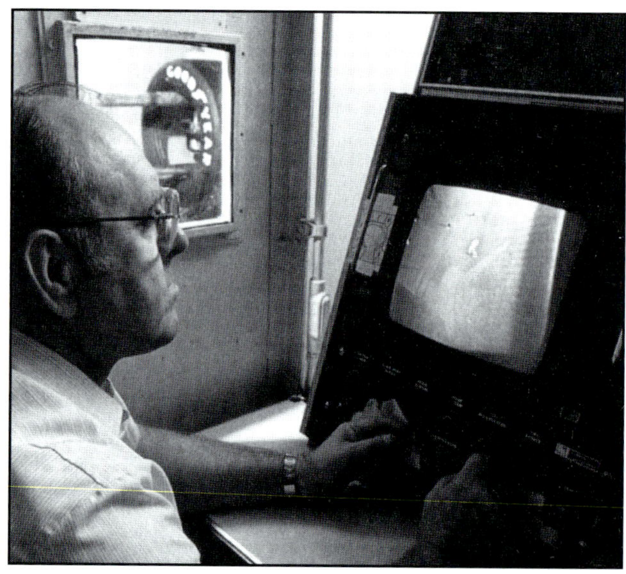

GOODYEAR

GOODYEAR

RACE INSPECT
GOODYEAR
GOODYEAR

law that prevented flights from leaving the airport after one a.m. It was almost 1:30 by the time we got the plane loaded, but they took off anyway," Gaug says with a very mischievous smile. "Guess our watches were slow."

They had already called customs at Bologna. Customs closed at midnight but they agreed to have someone back there by four a.m. to clear all the tires. The truck was to be there to meet the plane, and get the tires to the track by five a.m.

Oddly, everything worked like a well-oiled clock, which is unusual, especially since they had to deal with Italian Customs, which were renowned as being "difficult" at best. But the tires arrived, were cleared, loaded into the truck and were at the track by five on Sunday morning. At trackside, the whole Goodyear crew had worked at dismounting all the tires for every car in the field. They were ready for replacements.

"By the start of the race, each car had three sets of mounted tires," says Gaug. "Nelson Piquet won the race in a Williams Honda. Nobody had a tire problem all day."

That wasn't the only time there were problems. "We had another dilemma at Adelaide in practice for the Australian Grand Prix. The tires had been working perfectly until Nigel Mansell blew one. We checked all the tires and found that there was some heat build-up in the shoulder area, so we called all the teams together and said, 'The tires are suspect and we can't run them.' When everybody gasped, we told them, 'Don't worry, we'll have it worked out by tomorrow.' "

Everybody in racing had come to respect Goodyear's judgment. They were convinced that Goodyear would not run a tire that wasn't safe; they also knew that they would be as good as their word, so everybody went home on the night before the race and got a good night's sleep. Everybody, that is, but the Goodyear guys.

"Some of the tires were getting too hot, particularly if the car was running too much toe-out or too much negative camber. It wasn't really a problem but still there was far too much heat build-up in the shoulder area," Gaug admits. "So during the night, we shaved every tire at the track. By the next morning, we were ready and everything was resumed as if nothing had happened."

Keke Rosberg won in a Williams Honda. Again the race was run without incident. It further cemented Goodyear's relationship with race teams. The drivers and crews knew they could count on them.

A Team Williams Formula I car at speed. The Williams team and its drivers have worked closely with Goodyear in tire testing.

Formula I driver Keke Rosberg.

No longer were there days and weeks of frustration and agonizing over whether or not Goodyear would make the race; now the question was, "What do you do when you have no competition?"

The answer was simple: "In Formula I, for example, it was our policy that even though we had a monopoly, we would continue to improve our tires. Some European journalists said we would build a spec tire—the same for everybody, the same for every race—and let it go at that. Well, I can tell you, we never have. We're just as soft now and just as far out as if we were going up against other companies.

"Sure, there's not as much developing going on as if we had competition, but until we come up with a better construction, we are racing the best tire we can produce," Gaug says. "The guys are still working hard to make an even better one. We could make a spec tire—it would be much simpler—but the drivers wouldn't necessarily have the best. I promise you, they're going to have the best possible Goodyear race rubber."

Changes and Challenges

Motorsports is changing; not just the tire side of it, all of racing. Gone are the fun-loving days of NASCAR when drivers and crews partied into the wee, small hours the night before a race. There were times when they had to stop partying because the sun had come up—not that the sun coming up made all that much difference, but they had to go racing. And they did—they went out and drove like madmen.

"Some of the fun is gone," says Mike Babich, with a tinge of remorse in his speech. "Money is the big difference. The big sponsorships have converted the revelers to businessmen. Money does that."

Richard Petty is a living testimonial to how much the money picture has changed in racing. He won twenty-seven races during the 1967 NASCAR season and took home $130,275 in prize money. For one thing, there surely never will be another race driver who even comes close to winning twenty-seven major races in a single season, and if he did, he would need a Brinks armored truck to haul away his earnings.

In recent years, NASCAR drivers have won perhaps four or five races and have taken home far more than a million dollars. If they win the Winston Million and the championship, it could go as high as three million dollars. It's not only in stock car racing, but in every form of motorsports. The cars that once had nothing but a number on them—because it was a "gentleman's sport"—are so covered with corporate logos that it's difficult at times to tell what color the car is.

"They used to be a close group, the racers; a fraternity. Now they don't even talk much to each other for fear they might slip and give away a secret. The fun of winning is still there and the competition on the track is still as fierce," says Babich, "but the real down-to-earth good times are gone.

"There is a lot more professionalism today, I'll have to admit that. There are computers everywhere and engineers; there are suspension engineers and aerodynamic engineers and even engine engineers. In the old days, if a car didn't handle, the David Pearsons and the Cale Yarboroughs stayed out there and they *made* it handle. Today the driver brings the car back into the garage area and turns it over to a team of engineers to make it handle. They go straight to their computers and within minutes the changes are made.

"The crews don't communicate from team to team, but Goodyear is still on the man-to-man, grass roots level with *every* team," Babich explains. What Goodyear learned a long time ago is total honesty. Everything has always been above board, and you never tell one team what the other is doing. Even if it involves a tire problem.

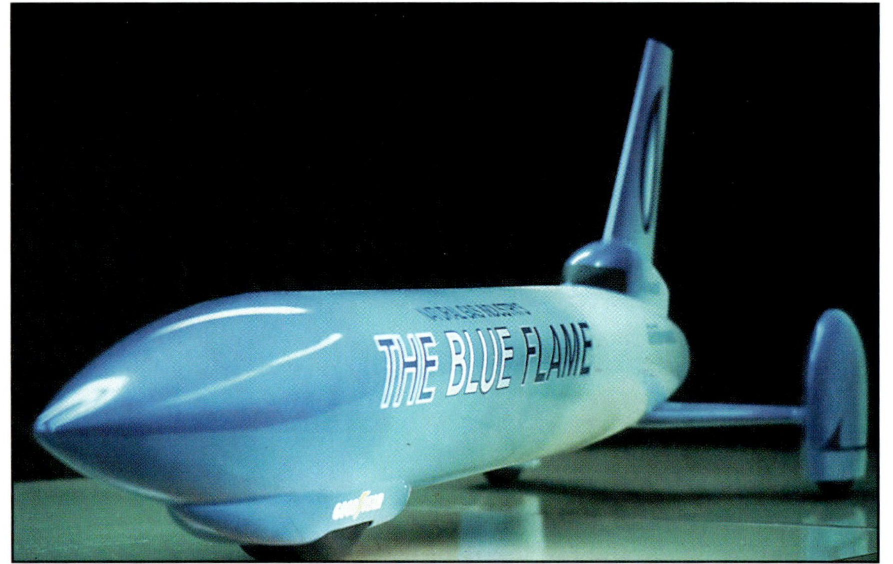

Gary Gabelich set a world land speed record of 622.407 mph on October 23, 1970 in the rocket-powered, liquified natural gas (LNG) fueled Blue Flame. *Goodyear tires carried the* Blue Flame *on its record-setting run. The* Blue Flame's *engine weighed only 770 pounds, yet could develop 58,000 horsepower. The project was managed by the Institute of Gas Technology.*

Dan Gurney at Indy. He was one of Goodyear's regular tire testers.

NASCAR action at Daytona in 1989.

Cut away of the Eagle GS-C.

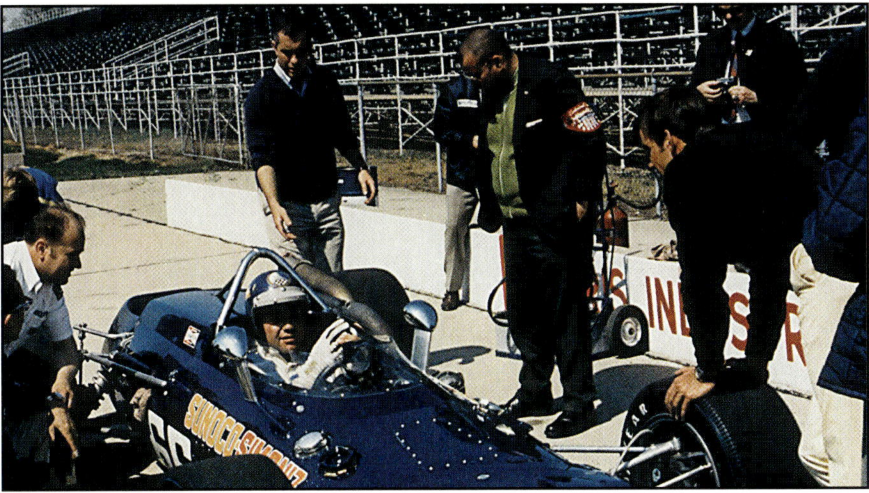

Mark Donohue in a 1969 Indy 500 practice session. Team-owner Roger Penske, behind car in sweater, offers his advice.

In the Cobra pits at the 12 Hours of Sebring, 1963. The farmers' overalls worn by Shelby's Cobra crews were a familiar sight at sports car events in the Sixties.

Mom and Pop Unser were a big part of racing in the Sixties, but son Al ran Firestones and son Bobby raced on Goodyears. The two p.r. guys from the tire companies got together and had a pair of "Goodstone" and "Fireyear" jackets made for the parents, both of whom are now deceased. Here they pose with their sons and Chuck Kerns, center, of Goodyear racing, at Indianapolis.

Two popular international drivers, Peter Revson, left, and Jack Brabham, prior to doing battle in the 1969 Indy 500. Revson started last, finished fifth; Brabham was forced out with ignition problems.

Gary Gabelich, far left, driver of the Blue Flame.

Racing tire, above left, with built-in "gutters" and "downspouts" to channel rainwater from underfoot, was developed by Goodyear in 1970 for USAC *road course events.*

Slick, fat and fast—Goodyear's 15-inch-wide 1972 Indy tire, above, had virtually no tread pattern; it rests on the 1971 Indy 500 tire: note differences in width and tread pattern from one year to the next.

Pat Clancy's six-wheeler, center, ran three times at Indianapolis, with Billy Devore's 12th place finish in 1948 being its best effort before Clancy gave up on the six-wheel idea. Twenty-eight years later, Derek Gardner and Ken Tyrrell came up with a Formula I race car for the 1976 season, left, with four tiny front wheels. Just goes to show that the "newest" ideas aren't always that new!

Goodyear's Leo Mehl, above, in a rare moment of relaxation at Indy '78.

Pre-race lap at the 1970 24 Hours of Daytona. (center)

A.J. Foyt, bottom right, with his 1977 Gilmore Racing Team Indy car in which he won his fourth Indy 500.

Dickie Smothers, below on left, with promoter Alec Ulmann after taking class win at Sebring '71. Ulmann had been an aeronautical engineer with Goodyear during World War II.

"You help the team that's having the problem with their suspension or whatever, but you never let anybody else know they've been having any trouble. You don't tell the other teams how this one team is able to run ten or twenty degrees cooler or whatever; the other teams never even know. You work out problems and solve them in silence, even though it might be a problem that has affected your tire.

"Even drag racing has changed, when you get to the pro ranks. Oh, some of the lower level classes resemble racing twenty-five years ago, but not the pros. They're as secretive as NASCAR or CART or Formula I."

The teams today in all forms of professional racing are almost totally on instrumentation. In the past few years, driver input appears to have diminished in setting up a car.

"There have been a few drivers in recent years that the guys running the computers still listen too, but very few," muses Babich. "Rick Mears was phenomenal that way and certainly A.J. Foyt. A.J., for instance, would let you know immediately what was wrong. He didn't need a computer, and, you know, I'll bet if you polled all of the engineers who worked with A.J.—and who had a disagreement with him regarding compound or stagger or almost anything affecting the car—they wouldn't know of a time when he wasn't right."

Foyt was beyond description. But then so were a lot of the early drivers who drove by the seats of their pants before computers took over.

"Today there are guys in each crew that do nothing but monitor the team effort," says Perry Bell, who is now chief engineer of the racing tire program. "They look at what is going on, talk to the crew chief and the driver and the computer experts. But the success Goodyear has had at the track didn't come as a result of computers.

"We were at trackside to help solve any problems before the race, because you don't want to get beat on when you're on the firing line. We differed from the other tire companies because we didn't wait until race day to send our engineers, otherwise it would have been an uphill battle of Perry Bell against Michelin. We did it all at test and practice sessions; the other guys did it at the track at race time.

"We made changes before we got there, so that gave us rapid response. I guess the biggest advantage we've had over the past three decades is our ability to respond to people who came up and tried to make a run at us. Traditionally we had designers and compounders side-by-side at tire tests. The same was true back at the plant. With the other companies, there was almost a wall between them.

"Our system had been built up that way from the beginning," Bell says. "You work together as a team and you end up with a lot better product. I think we've proved our point."

A good case in point is the battle with Hoosier in NASCAR. Hoosier is a tiny tire-maker in Lakeville, Indiana, that has supplied primarily dirt tires to racers over the years. When their enthusiasm led them to NASCAR, it became another tire war, not of the proportions of the Goodyear-Firestone war of two decades earlier, but enough to cause Goodyear to point its guns at the "intruder."

"Hoosier came out with a pretty good tire," admits Babich, "but it was because of NASCAR as much as anything else. They didn't want the cars to go any faster because they were having trouble with the high speeds. They wanted to restrict speed and threatened to reduce tire size. In reality this held down stock car tire development."

While all of this was happening, Hoosier hired Mike Hopkins away from Goodyear. He had been the company's chief engineer of race tire engineering. He was the man who set up Hoosier for its assault on the hallowed nest of the Eagle. He knew all of the Goodyear secrets, so he made it tough.

"The first thing we did was change compounds, to something he was not familiar with. It caused us some concern; he had been with us for ten years and he set them up with sound technology," says Babich. "The thing that hurt them most was that they placed the emphasis on a few teams and put most of their money in them. They played games, but it wasn't the first time that had happened to drivers. It was just that it hadn't happened for a couple of decades."

Reporters on the Winston Cup scene made it into hard news: "Small Independent Tire Maker Takes on Akron Giant!" It was expected; after all, the "David and Goliath" theme is a natural story line. It attracted attention even outside racing circles.

The struggle for world racing supremacy between Goodyear and Firestone in the mid-Sixties and early Seventies was a classic tire war. So too was the Goodyear-Michelin battle in Formula I that ran from 1978 until 1984. It was excellent news fodder—huge tire companies slugging it out on the race tracks of the world with performance, image and market share the ultimate prizes.

The protagonists in the latest war were two different animals, playing two different games. Measured by practically any yardstick you might choose, Goodyear was the Number One tire company in the world. Racing, to Goodyear, was high stakes activity, linking performance, engineering and sales in the competitive high-performance tire market, both original equipment and aftermarket.

Hoosier, on the other hand, had but one product—racing tires. So Hoosier, admittedly, was racing to beat Goodyear, because Goodyear was considered Number One in racing. It was that simple.

But the scales were way out of balance. Hoosier really had little on the line but pride. Goodyear had much more to lose than to gain. So how did this seemingly lopsided contest evolve?

During the 1986 takeover attempt by corporate raider James Goldsmith, rumors of the demise of Goodyear's racing program ran rampant. Although Goodyear was the sole supplier of Winston Cup tires and had worked tirelessly over the decades to supply them with the best possible product, rules did not exclude other tire companies from the series. Hoosier was a participant in the 1987 Busch Grand National series and its corporate request to run Winston Cup in 1988 was promptly approved by NASCAR.

With Goodyear surviving the takeover, it looked like the NASCAR tire dilemma was resolved. What no one took into consideration was that Hoosier might just take the Winston Cup business seriously, which is precisely what they did.

As an accommodation to NASCAR to keep speeds and costs under control, Goodyear developed a safe but not necessarily fast race tire. This was the tire Hoosier had to beat, and with one of Goodyear's own running the program it was not a particularly tough assignment.

Hoosier made a good showing in the first two races of the 1988 season, finally winning with Neil Bonnett's car at Rockingham, North Carolina. While Goodyear was eagerly looking for its 500th straight Winston Cup victory, Bonnett ended the winning streak at 464 and added fuel to the fire in the latest tire war.

In March, Goodyear decided it was time for a new Winston Cup tire. They had had enough. Within four days, the new tire, complete with a new mold, was ready. Two hundred of the new Eagles were built, cured

Stock car tire coming out of the curing press at Goodyear's Akron plant in 1975. The temperature of the race tire as it comes from the curing press is 310 degrees F., considerably hotter than the 260-degree tire temperatures reached at Daytona's Firecracker 400 each July 4th.

and shipped to the Atlanta International Raceway in Georgia where they were tested by three loyal Goodyear drivers: Dale Earnhardt, Rusty Wallace and Bill Elliott.

One thousand tires were ready for the *Atlanta Journal* 500 in late March. Forty of the forty-two starters rode on the new Eagle, including the man who dominated and won the race, Dale Earnhardt. The tire war wasn't over, but the Atlanta battle was a blow to Hoosier.

Racers, used to the old wear-resistant compounds, were in the habit of installing brand new "label" tires every pit stop and then running them hard. This built up a lot of heat fast. In simplest terms, the overheated tread surface "greased-up," causing the tire to gradually lose traction or "give-up," as the racers said.

At the Michigan International Speedway in late June, Goodyear introduced a new family of compounds. The Michigan tire not only was fast initially but wore effectively and exhibited very little "give-up."

During the second half of the season, Goodyear came back strong and the war seemed to be won. Hoosier continued for part of two seasons and finally withdrew. It had not been an easy struggle; Hoosier had put up a valiant effort, but Goodyear simply had too many guns. It is not to say, however, that Hoosier isn't working diligently in northern Indiana to ready another salvo at racing's Number One tire company.

Goodyear has learned to thrive on competition.

It has been an arduous climb but Goodyear has become the world standard of race tires

Radials had reached the top plateau in all forms of racing. So, too, had Goodyear. It had been a long, arduous climb to the zenith, but the fact that Goodyear was now the world standard of race tires made it all worthwhile. Leo Mehl was one of a handful of original men left in the racing division, and he looked with pride to the unbelievable success of the world's greatest racing force.

The first Indy car radial was the road course version that debuted at Portland, Oregon, in a race won by Al Unser, Jr. Every Indy car road course race since then has been run and won on Eagle race radials.

Stock car racing was the final bastion in which Goodyear offered radial race tires. Darrell Waltrip and the engineers, led by Greg Stucker and Rick Campbell, conducted the first tests at North Wilkesboro, North Carolina. Consequently, Waltrip won the first stock car race on radials in the International Race of Champions at Daytona in 1985.

From there it was all uphill: Dale Earnhardt won the first stock car circular race on the new radials at North Wilkesboro; Mario Andretti won the first oval Indy race on the new tires at Pocono and Al Unser, Sr., won his fourth Indianapolis 500 on them in 1987.

Bill Elliott, driving Junior Johnson's mount on Eagle radials, sped to victory in the final Winston Cup race of 1992. This Atlanta win was the 937th for Goodyear in Winston Cup competition. It, like Richard Petty's amazing 200 NASCAR wins, will undoubtedly stand for all time.

Confidence and Commitment

Chairman and CEO Stan Gault became the latest "man at the top" in Goodyear racing. He followed in the footsteps of those supportive chairmen who had preceded him. If anything, he was even more enthusiastic about the motorsports program than had been his predecessors.

"Over the years, once the board chairmen got used to life in the fast lane, they really got involved—from Russ DeYoung to Chuck Pilliod to Bob Mercer," says Walt DeVinney. "When the gauntlet was passed to Stan Gault, it was no different.

"I don't think any of them were particularly impressed until they became the top man and got to learn first hand the respect Goodyear is accorded when they visited the various tracks. More importantly, when they went to the races, they actually *saw* what was being accomplished.

"What they saw is their people getting things done fast and doing the impossible. It takes a racing mentality to accomplish this," explains DeVinney. "When reporters ask what we get out of racing, I always say, 'Material, development and production techniques.' But there also is people development. I mean, you have these people who are working directly with racers, but still they have instant feedback from the customers."

Leo Mehl, who has ruled the racing effort for about two decades, leans back in his office chair and stares straight into the tough but glorious past:

"Basically we started sticking a tire machine in here and one in

Pit action for Indy cars at Mid-Ohio road course in 1989.

Lee Gaug discusses tires in the pits at the Detroit Grand Prix.

there; we modified truck machines and existing tire apparatus and we did amazingly well with the make shift equipment. But when radials came along, we had to start from scratch. Now our biggest advantage is that this new, high-tech equipment is coupled with the experience of the world's best race tire production people. It had to be a winning combination.

"The main advantage we have had over our competition is that our engineering doesn't stop with the design and compound of tires. Our engineers are very conversant with what it takes to make a uniform tire, which, of course, is the key.

"Advancements between yesterday and today are mind-boggling," Mehl says with conviction. "First it was cut and try. We went to tests and learned by guess and by gosh and then, as a compounder, on the airplane home I dreamed up another dozen compounds. The next day we started working on them.

"As for lab tests, I didn't have a whole lot of confidence in them because it was very hard to relate the traction of a tread compound on the track with the traditional tests they used back in Akron for passenger tires. But it's all very sophisticated today; the computers have changed everything. You can actually design a tire and the computer will visualize the design, so you can take a look at it. It will show you what the tire will

Johnny Rutherford and his wife Betty (left foreground) in Victory Circle after Johnny won the 1980 Indy 500—making him a three-time Indy winner.Rutherford was one of Goodyear's earliest tire testers.

look like on the race track. "Our guys can do a great job in predicting what the speed is going to be and what the cornering forces will be. We can tell if the tire actually can handle the kind of load demanded on it by certain tracks. Before we were just winging it.

"It started to get a little more scientific in the mid-Seventies," recalls Mehl. "We spent lots of money computerizing data from our race tires. We had a giant truck full of high-tech equipment, so we had load sensors on the suspension and throttle response and loads on each corner of the car. We even hooked up the driver's blood pressure and heart beat. I think we did a lot of things that weren't pertinent to tire development, but we had all this sophisticated equipment, so why not use it?

"The only problem was that it was all so new to us—and to racing—that it took us three or four months to analyze the data. By then it was out of date. Today we can analyze it quickly," Mehl says. "Consequently we have even more confidence in our product."

Goodyear engineers not only have the ability to design a tire properly, but can identify where the edge is for safety. That's important to

Late Model (left) and Stock Car Goodyear Eagle racing tires—1992 versions.

the driver. And to Goodyear. They can look at load and heat characteristics—things they didn't know in the beginning until they crossed them.

The engineers are astonishing in predicting what a tire will do, even if someone builds a new circuit. They can tell what compound and what design for dry tracks and what tread for wet conditions. It all depends on load, and load depends on speed. They can now model a tire and design it for any track.

"Another thing, which is even amazing to me," admits Mehl, "is how much knowledge our engineers have of the car's suspension and to what is happening aerodynamically. You have to realize that we're dealing daily with the best car designers and builders in the world. Working with these guys on a day-to-day basis is something we have that nobody else has. It's great to watch our engineers give advice to world-class car builders.

"It's a lot more complex now. You can't just go out there and stand on it. I mean, when you're cornering at three or four Gs, you better know exactly what you're doing."

The technological advances are very important to Goodyear because the company makes about 450 different types of racing tires. They make that many more experimental tires so in the course of a year, perhaps 900 different types run through the Tech Center.

"Making sure we have enough tires for every stock car or Indy car or Formula I or drag race, for every Group C or dirt or short track race, makes you realize the great dedication and planning ability of our field managers and engineers and production guys," Mehl exclaims.

"But even though we tell a driver that we've got this great tire, it doesn't mean much to him until he wins with it. Over the years, we've

Goodyear's 1992 Short Track racing Eagle.

learned that the most important thing is having the product. There isn't even a close second. The reason we have been able to do this is because of Goodyear management. That's the bottom line." Mehl continues, "Every chairman we've ever had has been a tiger, and every one has hated to lose.

"The times we've lost, management has always asked, 'Why did you lose and what do you need to make sure it doesn't happen again?' It lets you know in no uncertain terms the object is to get out there and win."

Goodyear has worked with the most outstanding automotive people in the world in the past twenty-five years; it has provided not only their racing people but their management with an opportunity to get to know them and to nurture the relationship; it includes every major manufacturer in the world, from Ferrari to Mercedes to Jaguar, to Honda, Toyota, Nissan and Mazda, to Ford and Chevy and Chrysler. They deal with all of the great automotive personalities in the world.

Goodyear's philosophy is that when all of the great race drivers in the world are running your product, it can't help but improve relationships with the people who build the cars.

"If we started racing today," ponders Mehl, "we could never get this knowledge because the company couldn't afford to develop this kind of technology at today's prices. But we started when they started and we all learned, made mistakes, corrected them and went on to the next plateau. The key word is 'learned.'

"Our people had the intestinal fortitude to stick with it, even though there were times in the beginning when we weren't winning much. It's tough to work your tail off and then go out there and lose week after week; it takes some big men to say, 'to hell with it, we're going to whip this thing,' and then do it."

Technology Counts

"Protect Our Good Name" plaques have adorned Goodyear office walls as long as anyone can remember. The slogan never was forgotten by anybody in the racing division. In the company's long history, there certainly never had been a better way for Goodyear to protect its good name than through motorsports.

The fringe benefits are astounding. For example, in 1985 the Eagle line represented five percent of all Goodyear tire sales; by 1991, it had risen to thirty-five percent. Nobody argues the fact that racing was responsible.

"The race tire is the one thing that the teams can't duplicate," Mehl assures. "The top teams are spending between $20 and $140 million. They can create a complete engine, electronics, chassis, carbon fiber this and that. But the one thing they can't make is tires. And they don't like that; they would like to think of themselves as wholly independent and we're the only thing that's standing in the way of that claim.

"What is even more comforting to us is the fact that we have maintained a monopoly in high-performance tires for so many years; it's

The Monaco Formula I Grand Prix, 1990.

a phenomenal success story.

"There's nothing the manufacturers like better than having five or six suppliers for each item they have to buy," Mehl exclaims. "They like to have all these companies competing for their business, but with high-performance tires they virtually have but one—Goodyear."

The major thing Goodyear has to offer—whether it be at the track or at the original equipment level—is technology. What they referred to as "technology" in the Sixties and early Seventies was little more than trial-and-error, but the engineers are so advanced now that they know suspensions and do computer modeling; they can predict what a tire will do in any application.

"There was a time when the crews were reluctant to give us all the information on their cars," recalls Mehl. "They were paranoid about everything because they weren't any more sure about it than we were. But all of that has changed with the great strides in technology. Over a long period of time, they have learned that they can trust us with their most secret information. It goes no farther than our engineers."

It took a lot of time, effort and money to get Goodyear to this point. "We have earned our technical leadership by investing millions of dollars in production facilities and race tire engineering technology. It's been costly. The equity that Goodyear has built from its racing program is priceless," states Mehl.

A Cold Indy

Goodyear was ready with more new ideas for highway and track—they introduced them in 1992.

"We launched our new yellow-lettered tires and our Z-rated Eagle

Sideview of the 1993 Hall-VDS Pennzoil Special, a Lola T9300 with Chevrolet V8-C engine.

Cut away of the 1991 Hall-VDS Pennzoil Indy car.

From the left: NASCAR Winston Cup Drivers Terry LaBonte, Sterling Marlin, Dale Jarrett and Bill Elliott.

GA, which is probably the most popular tire we've ever made," says Fred Kovac.

"The Cadillac Allante Indy Pace Car had them. We also unveiled our tubeless inner-shield tire. Of course, we've had the inner tire for twenty-five years, but this new one was even better. To balance out the road and track picture, we brought out a high-performance snow tire.

"Racing has become so integral to our way of thinking that I don't believe we could develop the kind of passenger car tires that we have in recent years without it. The Eagle has become synonymous with performance."

But all was not particularly rosy for the yellow-lettered Eagles during the 1992 Indy race. For several days before, the weather had been warm. But race day dawned cold and blustery. It was the coldest Indianapolis race day in recorded history.

More of today's drivers, left to right: Ernie Irvan, Rusty Wallace and Dale Earnhardt of NASCAR's Winston Cup circuit, and Fermin Velez, driver in the IMSA Camel Lights events.

Nobody thought there would be such a severe weather change overnight. It was a shift the likes of which not even the old-timers had remembered seeing at Indy.

"We had two types of tires there, the one we expected to race and a backup in case it got unusually *hot*," says Mehl. "Heat is normally the problem, but that morning it was forty-eight degrees."

Goodyear had grave concerns about the weather. Obviously the drivers needed to get the tires heated up before they really got on it, but it's hard to convince any race driver to hold back. Besides, the cars simply don't run well at slow speeds because the wings and body don't give proper ground effects at slow speeds and the air is "dirty" from other

Three campaigners in the IMSA Camel GTP series: left to right, Juan Manual Fangio II, namesake and nephew of the famed Fangio of the '50s and '60s; P.J. Jones, son of Parnelli; and David Tennyson.

cars being so close. They are balanced to run at 220 mph or more at Indy. Anything less and you've got a car that doesn't handle properly.

"The car isn't very nice at slower speeds," says Stu Grant. "Now, suddenly, you've got a lot of caution flags and these guys are having to run slowly; that, as much as anything else, was responsible for the many accidents.

"If the drivers had held back to even 200 [mph] and put up briefly with an ill-handling car, one that was a little on the loose side, it would have helped. The car would have been squirrely, but they could have handled it.

"There was some discussion as to whether or not the cars should have changed tires after some of the crashes, which often brought out the yellow four or five laps after the green flag had been given to the field, but because of the many crashes, they wanted as much rubber on the track surface as possible to protect them if they ran over something.

"There was a lot of debris and a lot of tires with small cuts in them that nobody in the stands knew anything about. Michael Andretti got away well every time," says Grant, "but he was one of the few. Several others left the pits and spun right into the wall, bringing out even more caution flags."

"Some of the guys used their heads and didn't charge into the corner as fast," says Mehl, "and the guy behind him thought, 'hell, maybe I can catch him,' and he stood on it. It was a *Catch 22* situation; if they *did* charge they spun, if they didn't somebody spun into *them*. Mario Andretti, a real veteran, told me simply, 'I should have known better.' "

Al Unser, Sr., said, "Tom Sneva went charging past me and I thought, 'There's no way he's gonna' make that corner on those cold tires.' And, sure enough he hit the wall."

Experienced drivers were in a situation they hadn't been in before. "Maybe the drivers should have held back, but it's hard for them to do that," says Mehl. "In the Seventies or Eighties we had compounds that wouldn't come on until after several laps and they got warmed up. Everybody knew that and they were really careful. Our recent compounds at Indy warm up more easily—however, Race Day 1992 was the coldest start in history at Indy."

Reporters said there should have been more warm-up laps after each yellow flag. They should have dropped the green and held the cars to 200 mph or less; to turn them loose on cold tires was asking for trouble, they postulated. Maybe they were right.

Nobody blamed Goodyear. Everybody knew that even with all of their positive attitude and super planning, there was absolutely nothing

Today's Drivers

Heading into the mid-Nineties are a talented group of drivers in all forms of auto racing.

A few of those, some familiar and some new, are pictured on these pages—selected not for their individual accomplishments but as representatives of the whole.

The Blimps

The Goodyear blimp is an anticipated sight at most major racing events.

Spectacular in its own right, the blimp is particularly appreciated by the media, who otherwise would not have a position from which to obtain overall or broadview photos of the race scene below.

Though Goodyear manufactured its first blimp on May 30, 1917, under government contract—it was not until the Thirties that Goodyear recognized its promotional possibilities and the blimp soon became Goodyear's hallmark. With the onset of World War II, Goodyear's existing blimps were requisitioned by the government and additional blimps manufactured for war-time use. Following the war, Goodyear bought

Cars run under the Goodyear bridge and into the night at Sebring, 1972.

five blimps back from the government.

By 1958, the Mayflower, *based in Miami, was Goodyear's last blimp. At this point Bob Lane was hired on as Director of Public Relations. Recognizing the tremendous p.r. potential, he asked for more blimps. In 1963, the* Columbia *joined the* Mayflower, *with* America *complimenting the fleet in 1965. In 1972 blimp activities expanded to Europe with the* Europa.

Distinctly visible by day, a spectacular 'sign in the sky' at night, the Goodyear blimp has been a familiar sight not only at races but at all types of major sports and special events.

A card-carrying guest, Mayflower, *1963, Sebring*

Left page, top: the Goodyear blimp displays its new paint scheme.

Center, an example of the spectacular light shows provided by the blimp at night.

Bottom, far left, a cut away of the new yellow-lettered Goodyear Eagle racing tire, and to its right a pair of racing Eagles on display.

that they could do about the weather. It was a crash-marred race, but nobody was critically injured, and that's always the important thing, to Goodyear and everybody else involved in motorsports. After all, cars can be replaced.

There was no doubt that had the weather been even ten degrees warmer, the tires would have worked fine, the drivers could have charged all day and it's possible that it could have been one of the safest races instead of the demolition derby it turned out to be. But that's racing. And it's what one has to expect. Some days you eat the bear...

More than 221 Miles Per Hour

An important event happened at Indianapolis in 1993, one that caused Goodyear's racing people to look back fondly to a time exactly thirty years earlier when Anthony Joseph Foyt, Jr., had called Goodyear to "come on down" to Indy. "Super Tex," at age 58 and with thirty-five Indy 500s behind him, climbed into his trusty Number 14 race car, turned a lap at more than 221 miles per hour—possibly fast enough to put him on the front row—and then he pulled into the pits and announced his retirement from racing.

A.J. Foyt as team manager at Indy 1993.

It was precisely what one would have expected from this world's greatest racer. He wanted everybody to know that he was retiring because he *wanted* to, not because he *had* to.

As Goodyear's chief tester for three decades, Foyt's contributions to Goodyear's success were immeasurable.

Number One in Racing

Goodyear is at the top of the heap now, and it looks as if they intend to stay there. Sure, there will be challenges from companies like Michelin and maybe Bridgestone or even Hoosier, but you can bet the Akron clan will be ready. In fact, they welcome the confrontation.

As Goodyear begins its fifth decade of racing in the modern era, and their third of domination of the sport, they look with pride to their new slogan: "Goodyear. #1 in Racing; Goodyear. #1 in Tires."

With Goodyear on the scene, records have fallen in every form of motorsports: Indianapolis cars are going well over 225 miles per hour, stock cars are over 200, Kenny Bernstein broke the magical 300-mile-per-hour mark in the quarter-mile in drag racing, Formula I cars handle as if they were on rails. The list is endless. The accolades beyond belief.

The flight of the Eagle has been magnificent. Many of the original players are gone. They're watching from a better and safer vantage point. The few who remain look fondly over their shoulders at what assuredly is the greatest period of accomplishment in the history of the sport. They're still out of breath from constantly running flat-out for the past thirty years, but they have protected their good name. And they've done it with a style and perseverance no one has ever seen in any sport.

It is a class act.

Goodyear truly is the "greatest name in rubber."

International, CART, Daytona, Indy '93 and A View from the Other Side

Silverstone, 1992. Formula I cars bunch up through a turn in the British Grand Prix.

Goodyear rain tires doing their job at the Suzuka circuit in Japan during the 1992 Formula I event.

The Start of the 1992 Australian Grand Prix for Formula I cars.Every car in the race is running on Goodyears.

The sparks from this Formula I car add drama to an already exciting event at Monza, Italy in 1992. Because of the low clearance, cars can bottom out on rough spots on the race course.

The Start of the Portuguese Grand Prix at Estoril, 1992. Notice the uphill grade as they go into the turn.

And it was rain in Spain for the 1992 Formula I race at Barcelona.

Leo Mehl, left, and Bobby Rahal share a laugh at Mid-Ohio in 1990.

The race car of Davey Allison is pushed toward the pits at the 1993 Daytona 500. In the background can be seen the Goodyear Tower.

A fresh batch of racing Eagles at Daytona in 1993.

A typical pit scene at the Daytona 500 in 1993 (above left).

Goodyear Chairman and CEO Stanley Gault and his wife tour the garage area at Daytona in 1993.

On the front row at Indy '93, all sporting yellow-lettered Goodyear Eagles: Car 9, Raul Boesel, finished 4th; Car 6, Mario Andretti, finished 5th; and Car 10, Arie Luyendyk, finished 2nd.

Goodyear board chairman Stan Gault, right, discussing the company's Indy car tires with race director Leo Mehl in the paddock at the 1989 Mid-Ohio CART *race.*

Some of the tires required to run the 1993 Indy 500.

Pit action at the 1993 Indianapolis 500.

Holding up two fingers to signify his second Indianapolis 500 victory, Emerson Fittipaldi radiates the joy of every Indy winner. Breaking with tradition, "Emmo," owner of substantial orange groves, reached for the orange juice before accepting the traditional bottle of Indiana milk. In the right corner is a very happy Mrs. Fittipaldi.

Fittipaldi wears the familiar blue Goodyear hat signifying that this race was won on Goodyear tires. His car was a Penske 93 Chevrolet/C.

A View from the Other Side

That's pretty much the story. The dust has settled from the early skirmishes between Goodyear and Firestone and there simply aren't many people left who really remember those days. It all has changed so much.

In those early days not many Goodyear guys talked to their Firestone counterparts. After all, it was war and everybody knows you don't fraternize with the enemy.

But everyone, including the Goodyear guys, had a lot of respect for Firestone's racing p.r. man, Humphrey "Humpy" Wheeler, now president of Charlotte Motor Speedway in North Carolina.

Nobody ever tried harder than Humpy to convince the media that Firestone was supreme. It seems fitting to hear his comments. It is, after all, how he and the rest of the competition felt about the good ol' days and the good ol' Goodyear boys:

"I always thought [Goodyear] was very professional. My first observation of them was in 1959 when, as a college student working part-time at the Darlington Raceway, I was asked to show Tony Webner, Goodyear's first racing director, around the track.

Humphrey Wheeler, President, Charlotte Motor Speedway.

"I didn't know it at the time, but that was the beginning of the Tire Wars. And I certainly didn't expect to be smack dab in the middle of it someday, but when I graduated from the University of South Carolina, I eventually wound up at Firestone as manager of racing public relations.

"I don't think the people at Firestone took Goodyear very seriously until 1965, mainly because they had limited success in NASCAR *and none at Indy," Wheeler recalls as he looks over his shoulder at a Firestone place in racing history which has diminished with the passing of time.*

"But in 1965, we took notice that this was going to be a real threat to us. You see, the month of June was when we got our biggest advertising and marketing boost—it was when the Firestone Indy ad ran all over the country.

"Since nobody from Firestone ever worked for Goodyear or vice versa *at that time, secrets were easier to keep. But, all of a sudden, we began to see some awfully smart Goodyear engineers showing up at the track." Wheeler becomes pensive. "We had that tremendous onslaught from Goodyear. It just kept coming. We always hoped it would stop and they wouldn't come back the next season, but there was a tenaciousness that kept pushing ahead on their part.*

"We began to see the handwriting on the wall, that this was going to be a long hard fight, and it was," Wheeler admits. "I can remember the day it all died: It was 1969 and I was on a fishing pier on North Carolina's Outer Banks when a local cop searched me out and told me that 'Bill McCrary wants you in Akron. Tomorrow.' I didn't know who had died, but I was there the next day.

"That's when Bill announced that Firestone was going to continue racing, but we were going to do it at our own terms. We were cutting all the drivers and teams off the lucrative contracts we had with them. We were going to make racing pay its own way.

"I knew it would never work," confides Wheeler, "but even then they couldn't believe that Goodyear wouldn't stop. It had been unbelievable; they kept beating [our] people that knew more about race tires than anybody in the history of the world. It wasn't too long after that when everybody in the racing business knew that Goodyear had won the war.

"Some of our guys said they had bought *it, but we knew that they had to make great technical advances to get where they were. They made the advances to keep the drivers happy, particularly A.J. Foyt.*

"When you get right down to it, Foyt was the worst thing that ever happened to Firestone and the best thing that ever happened to Goodyear, because he was so stubborn at that point that he wouldn't put up with anything less than perfection. There was not another race driver in America who put that much pressure on a tire company—never before and certainly never since.

"In one way they took the toughest person they could find and pleased him and, in so doing, won the battle."

That was a long time ago and, as we have said, things have changed a lot. He views Goodyear's ascent objectively:

"Leo [Mehl] and I had a couple of run-ins over the years but I respected him and all of the Goodyear effort," says Wheeler. "But Goodyear was having trouble at Charlotte a couple of years ago in our May race. Hoosier was nipping at their heels and, to make matters worse, the Goodyear tires didn't seem to be working. Leo

flew down from Indianapolis to see if he could quell the storm.

He came straight to my office.

"I said to him, 'Leo, we have to help you get out of this mess,' and then I took him over to the pits to talk to the drivers. The first one we ran into was Dale Earnhardt, who has always been one of Goodyear's strongest supporters. Earnhardt sensed what Leo was considering [pulling the tires from the race] and he said, 'Well, hell, I'm gonna' run your tires. You're not going to pull out.'

"Most of the top drivers did *run Goodyears that day and I think it helped with the company's morale. Leo said to me, 'I always thought up to this moment that you were still working for Firestone and that you didn't like us.' I said, 'Leo, that's not true. That's ghosts from the past. I've exorcised them.'*

"But look at the situation today: Considering the fact that Firestone has been sold to the Japanese and Goodyear is still right in the thick of racing, it's pretty extraordinary because Goodyear is one of the few companies in the American automobile business that has not succumbed to the Japanese.

"Again the tenacity has come forth; that's what I think is the greatest virtue that Goodyear as a company has displayed over the years. They have been brainy, but the Japanese and the Europeans have been just as brainy. The tenacity has made the difference, and I don't know where it came from; maybe it's part of the Buckeye culture, I don't know," Wheeler contemplates.

"Here's a good example of the respect Goodyear built up in a relatively short time: It was the 1964 Daytona 500...Richard Petty was running well, but I saw that he had blistered a tire when he came in for his first pit stop. I went to the pits to talk to Lee [Petty] and Maurice [Richard's brother] about switching to Firestone. They wouldn't consider it. When he came in the next time with another blistered tire, I appealed to them again. They wouldn't budge.

"On the third stop with a blistered left rear, I talked directly to Richard—of course, we all could still hear *then. I said 'You really need to switch these things; you're never going to win this race until you do,' but he said 'No, they'll come around.' I didn't understand what he meant, but he stuck with Goodyear and won his first of seven Daytona 500s.*

"I saw him two weeks later in Richmond [Virginia] and I asked him why in the world he had stayed on those tires. He looked me straight in the eye and said, 'Because the Goodyear engineers told me that if the things started blistering, I could feel it in plenty of time to come in. The deal was, I was getting a pit stop out of them anyway and they were giving me fair warning, so I really just took their word for it and it all worked out.'

"He then went on to tell me that they had set up the car on Goodyears and if they had switched to Firestones, it would have upset the handling characteristics of the car. I said, 'You mean you really believed in those guys that much,' and he said, 'Absolutely.'

"It was this kind of faith the drivers had in Goodyear that kept them going. You had to respect what they were doing."

Humpy Wheeler

May of 1993: Bridgestone/Firestone of Japan announced that they were returning to Indy racing and would compete at the 1995 Indianapolis 500—the **TIRE WARS** *resume.*

Stanley Gault, Chairman of the Board and Chief Executive Officer, Goodyear Tire & Rubber Company.

There is no popular sport as global in its appeal as auto racing. And, as this book makes vividly clear, there is no sport that is so dependent on the complex mathematics and chemistry that go into the design and manufacture of tires.

The competitive instincts of Goodyear and its people, and their insatiable desire to be the best, provide *Tire Wars* its emotion and its conflicts on a worldwide stage—ideal casting for the ageless drama of men, women and machines pushing the edge of the envelope to new frontiers.

The return on Goodyear's considerable investments in auto racing over the years comes in as many shapes, shades and sizes as racing events and race machines themselves.

This book speaks eloquently of the competitive zeal auto racing nurtures, and how Goodyear associates cherish every checkered flag in which they share. That zeal and pride translate directly to competition for customers in every free market of the world.

The ultimate payoff goes to the customer who can buy Goodyear tires knowing that there is something in them that results from meeting the tough, unique and exacting demands of the race track...demonstrated publicly before millions of spectators week after week...and counted on for their performance and safety by the world's leading drivers.

Since I became CEO of Goodyear in mid-1991, I've literally traveled the globe as it's defined by Goodyear's tire markets and, of course, auto racing achievements. From Formula I to all classes of sports car victories, auto racing has further deepened the pride held by Goodyear associates in their company.

Auto racing victories give tangible dimensions to their competitive spirit and morale. Racing jackets and racing hats proudly display the Goodyear logo for associates at work, on ballfields and in the streets and backyards of their neighborhoods. The desire to identify with Goodyear as a winner rivals that of a soccer fan whose team snared the World Cup, or a football fan whose team just won the Super Bowl.

Tire Wars by Bill Neely is indeed a story about Goodyear victories in auto racing. More important, though, it is another deserved tribute to the men and women of Goodyear, to those involved in race tire development, engineering, manufacturing and distribution—and equally to those who might never see or touch a race tire—for their endless contributions to company success.

Stan Gault

GOODYEAR.
RACING TO BRING YOU THE BEST TIRES IN THE WORLD.
GOODYEAR
EAGLE
GOODYEAR

M

N

O

P

Q

R

S